THE CONSTANTINE GROUP

by
H. S. Appleyard

Published by the World Ship Society
Kendal LA9 7LT
1983

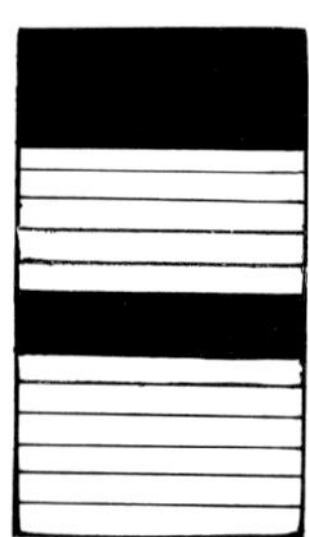

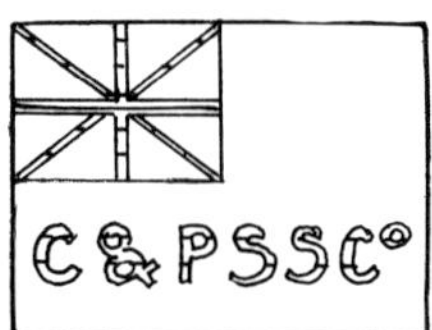

Constantine & Pickering
S.S. Co.

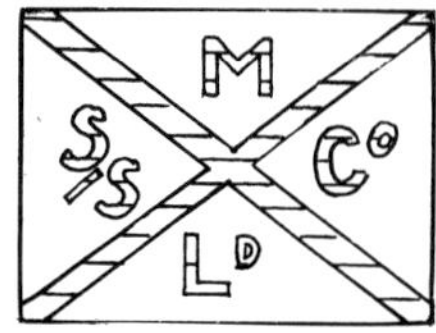

Meteor S.S. Co. Ltd.

Joseph Constantine
S.S. Line Ltd.

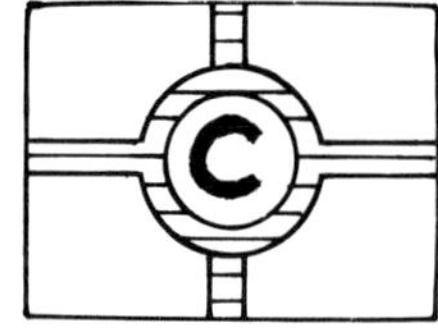

Constantine Sg. Co. Ltd.
Constantine Lines Ltd.

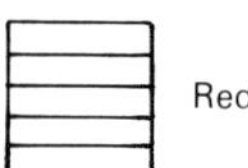

Red

ACKNOWLEDGEMENTS

The author wishes to acknowledge the assistance given by Mr. I. Chadwick of Constantine Holdings Ltd. He also wishes to acknowledge the assistance given by Lloyd's Register of Shipping, Messrs. M. Crowdy, R. Fenton and the World Ship Society Central Record Team.

The photographs were kindly provided as acknowledged in the history and the cover was designed by Mr. T. Adams.

ISBN 0 905617 24 X

Although belonging to an old Yorkshire family, Joseph Constantine was born in 1856 at Flensburg which was then Danish territory. His father was one of the managers of the British company which operated the railway in Schleswig but when Germany invaded Schleswig — Holstein the Constantine family returned to England and settled in Middlesbrough. On leaving school Joseph Constantine was apprenticed to Warley Pickering and Company, a firm of compass manufacturers and ship-chandlers in Middlesbrough. It was whilst employed by this firm that he invested in shares in a number of vessels, usually brigs which were owned on the sixty four share system.

It was in 1885 that Joseph Constantine and Warley Pickering Jnr. invested in the barque HOMEWOOD which at the time was trading under the Norwegian flag. She remained under the Norwegian flag but was managed from the Middlesbrough office with Captain Klaveness as her nominal owner. In 1887 a similar arrangement was made when the barque P. G. CARVILL was acquired and renamed NORWOOD. This vessel cost £4,500 of which over half was put up by Joseph Constantine and Warley Pickering whilst other members of the Constantine family also took shares. These two sailing ships traded successfully but the partners realised that the days of big profits were coming to an end and that the future lay in the steamship.

The first steamer to join the fleet was in 1891 when the SANTORIN was purchased, renamed TOFTWOOD and like the two sailing ships was registered under the Norwegian flag. In 1892 the steamers CRAIGHILL and BRITANNIA were acquired and renamed COPSEWOOD and WESTWOOD respectively. The fleet expanded further so that by 1896 it totalled six steamers and the two barques, all of which were registered in Norway. It was not uncommon for British owners to operate their ships under the Norwegian flag during this period but whatever the reasons were, the Company ceased to put any further ships on the Norwegian register after 1896. In 1897 the decision was taken to build up a fleet under the British flag with the purchase of the steamer SAM HANDFORD which was renamed RIFTSWOOD.

The managers since 1894 had been known as Messrs. Constantine and Pickering but as the business grew it was decided in 1897 to change the title to Constantine, Pickering and Company. Joseph Constantine's brother William was now acting as superintendent and supervised the building of new vessels. William Constantine was registered as managing owner of the BLAKEMOOR which was acquired in 1900 and renamed ROSEWOOD. The shipowning and ship-chandlery businesses continued to operate from the office in Dock Street, Middlesbrough but in 1901 the name was changed to the Constantine and Pickering Steamship Company whilst the ship-chandlery business continued to trade as Constantine, Pickering and Company.

As the fleet of ocean-going ships increased the Meteor Steamship Co. Ltd. was formed in 1907 to own coasting and short-sea ships. This company was managed by Messrs. R. A. Constantine and T. H. Donking who was a cousin of Mr. Warley Pickering. The first ship of this company was the CEDARWOOD of 1907 and she was followed in 1908 by the COPSEWOOD which had been building "on spec" in Sunderland. Two second-hand steamers were acquired in 1908 and joined the deep-sea fleet. These were the PURITAN and LINDENHALL but neither ships were renamed and in 1912 the LINDENHALL was sold back to her original owners. In 1910 the BIRCHWOOD was built for the Birchwood Steamship Co. Ltd. and was the only ship to be owned by this company which was managed by W. and W. W. Constantine. At this time it was decided to sell the original ship-chandlery business which was purchased by Furness, Withy and Co. Ltd. and continued to trade as Maritime Stores Ltd.

When the First World War broke out in 1914 the fleet consisted of 21 ocean-going steamers and six coastal vessels. During the early stages of the war three ocean-going vessels and three coasters were delivered and in addition three coasters were acquired. The Company was to lose 13 ships as a direct result of enemy action and a further 12 ships were sold. The PARKWOOD was wrecked in 1915 whilst returning from Archangel and the LARCHWOOD was sunk in collision off Bull Point in 1916. The elderly steamers TEESWOOD and ROSEWOOD were sunk as blockships by The Admiralty at Scapa Flow and when hostilities ceased only six ships remained from a combined fleet of 35 vessels. Although the loss of ships was disastrous the loss of life was remarkably light. The LOCHWOOD and THORPWOOD were sunk in 1915 without any crew being lost. In 1916 six men were lost when the CEDARWOOD was mined and sunk off Aldeburgh. The heaviest loss of life occurred when the MORDENWOOD was sunk in the Mediterranean with only eight survivors from her crew of 29. Two days after Christmas 1916 the COPSEWOOD was sunk without loss of life. In 1917 two men were lost when the BROOKWOOD sank and three crew did not survive when the QUEENSWOOD was attacked and sunk by a German submarine off Hartland Point. The TOFTWOOD, WARLEY PICKERING, BILSWOOD, MAPLEWOOD and GOODWOOD were lost but their crews were all saved. When the BIRCHWOOD was mined and sunk in 1918 there was again no loss of life.

In 1918 Mr. Warley Pickering had retired from the business and in 1920 the Joseph Constantine Steamship Line Ltd. was registered with a paid up capital of £999,900, virtually all of which was held by Mr. Joseph Constantine and his family. The years 1921 to 1923 saw the further decline of the fleet with the sale of ships which had survived the war and second-hand tonnage which had been purchased shortly after hostilities had ended. The coaster TRENTWOOD was sold to the newly formed Donking Steamship Co. Ltd., which was owned by Mr. T. H. Donking and Mr. Warley Pickering. In 1922 the steamer RONALEE was purchased and renamed MAPLEWOOD. This vessel and the WEARWOOD of 1912 were the only ships owned by the Joseph Constantine Steamship Line Ltd. at this time. Since 1909 the Company had been represented in London by its own office and staff but in 1921 Joseph Constantine and Sons (London) Ltd. was established to carry on the brokerage and agency work in the capital.

In 1922 the founder, Mr. Joseph Constantine, died at Northallerton. He had been made High Sheriff of Yorkshire in 1916 and had carried out a great deal of public work for the county and his town of Middlesbrough. He left legacies to benevolent institutions in which he had been keenly interested during his life. Among these, perhaps the most conspicuous was the Constantine Technical College, which he had established in Middlesbrough to provide facilities for technical education for all the industries associated with the district, including shipbuilding, engineering, metallurgy, chemistry and electrical work. After his death he was succeeded by his two sons, Robert Alfred Constantine and William Whitesmith Constantine, who became the firm's joint managers.

By 1923 steps had been taken to rebuild the fleet to its former strength. Two second-hand steamers were acquired and the coasters LEVENWOOD, LARCHWOOD and COPSEWOOD were delivered. They were followed by the deep-sea steamer QUEENSWOOD and in 1927 the HOMEWOOD and HAZELWOOD joined the fleet. The deep-sea fleet was further strengthened by the delivery of eight new ships by 1930 whilst seven new short-sea vessels were delivered by 1937. The HAZELWOOD and KIRNWOOD were withdrawn from service and fitted with Maierform bows which were to prove so successful in service that the next three ships were built with that style of bow.

These three ships were completed during 1936 and 1937 by Hawthorn, Leslie and Co. Ltd. at Hebburn on Tyne for the Constantine Shipping Co. Ltd. The WINDSORWOOD was completed in June 1936 and had the distinction of being the first ship in Britain to be built with the Maierform bow. A month later the YORKWOOD was completed and she was followed in February 1937 by the BALMORALWOOD. The trio were remarkable vessels and one of their most striking features was the high standard of accommodation provided for the twelve passengers, the officers and the crew. The passenger cabins, eight single and two double berth, were in a house at the fore-end of the promenade deck. Below them, the dining saloon and smoke room, both large for a cargo ship, were adjacent to one another looking forward. The officers had their accommodation amidships, the petty officers and ratings aft. The holds were clear with large 'tween decks for general and bulky cargo and were fitted with shifting boards for the carriage of grain. In addition each ship was equipped with about 8,000 cubic feet of refrigerated cargo space.

WINDSORWOOD *World Ship Photo Library*

The three ships traded regularly from Swansea and Port Talbot to Quebec and Montreal when the St. Lawrence was free from ice. During the season when the St. Lawrence was closed they sailed to South Africa, Mauritius, Australia and the River Plate. The Company came to an agreement with the National Gypsum Company and persuaded the Canadian Government to dredge and build a pier at the tiny port of Cheticamp, Cape Breton. This enabled ships to load cargo under the chutes and so obtain a monopoly of a very profitable trade. Plans were in hand to do the same at Dingwall, Cape Breton but the work was not completed until after the outbreak of war and by then the ships were no longer available to take advantage of it.

KINGSWOOD following the explosion   *Company Archives*

The auxiliary boiler secured for the tow   *Company Archives*

It was not only the new ships which attracted publicity in 1937 as much attention was drawn to the epic tow of the steamer KINGSWOOD from Australia to the River Tyne. The KINGSWOOD had been at anchor off Port Pirie prior to loading a cargo of zinc concentrates when on 3rd January 1937 a violent explosion occurred in the engineroom. The donkey boiler had exploded and the force of the explosion had blown the boiler through the watertight bulkhead at the after end of No. 2 hold, through a wooden partition bulkhead in No. 2 hold and carried away the centre line bulkhead between Nos. 2 and 3 hatchways. It continued its path through the watertight bulkhead at the after end of No. 1 hold and through the collision bulkhead at the forward end of No. 1 hold before entering the forepeak where it penetrated the shell plating on the starboard side just above the waterline. The boiler had travelled approximately 164 feet and had left a trail of damage throughout the ship which was now totally immobilised. It was decided to effect temporary repairs in Australia sufficient for towage to the United Kingdom where permanent repairs would be carried out. Arrangements were made with L. Smit en Co's Internationale Sleepdienst of Rotterdam who sent their tug GANGES to the scene. On 27th April the GANGES sailed from Port Pirie with the KINGSWOOD in tow and eventually arrived in the River Tyne on 14th September having towed the damaged steamer over 11,000 miles without incident.

A short-sea vessel which aroused some interest at this time was the motorship EDENWOOD. A self trimming collier, the EDENWOOD had been designed for the coal trade from the River Tyne which had hitherto been the stronghold of steam colliers. Special attention had been given to her accommodation and with her diesel propulsion she was one of the first motorships to be employed in the coal trade on a regular basis.

Shortly before the outbreak of the Second World War the Company moved to its present headquarters at York House, Borough Road, Middlesbrough. In 1939 the Company took over the management of the four coasters owned by the Northwest Shipping Co. Ltd. of Workington and as the war progressed a number of ships were managed on behalf of the Ministry of War Transport as well as for foreign owners whose country had been occupied. The Company's own fleet consisted of nine coastal and nine deep-sea ships, the latter having all been fitted with accommodation for twelve passengers.

NORTHWOOD at Poole in June 1939   *T. R. Griffin*

The first casualty occurred on Christmas Eve 1939 when the EDENWOOD was sunk in collision off the Nab Tower. In June 1940 the BALMORALWOOD and WINDSORWOOD were torpedoed and sunk within eleven days of each other in the North Atlantic and in August 1940 the BROOKWOOD was sunk. The KIRNWOOD was lost in December 1941 having survived two previous attacks on earlier voyages. The YORKWOOD was sunk off the Brazilian coast by a German submarine whilst sailing in ballast and in December 1943 the KINGSWOOD was lost. The short-sea fleet was particularly liable to attack by enemy aircraft or E-boats but only the LINWOOD and AVONWOOD were lost in November and December 1942 respectively.

MAPLEWOOD in wartime   *Brownell Collection*

The ships which survived also saw action on frequent occasions. The WEARWOOD was damaged in March 1941 during an air raid on Liverpool and in January 1940 the NORTHWOOD had been attacked by aircraft off Whitby. The LEVENWOOD was at the evacuation of Dunkirk and the PARKWOOD had to be towed back to Plymouth after the German raid at Granville. The BRIARWOOD transported men and stores of the British

Expeditionary Force to St. Nazaire and later was the last British ship to leave Narvik before it fell to German forces. In May 1940 she was attacked by a submarine in the North Atlantic whilst sailing unescorted. She escaped from the submarine and later during the same voyage brought down an enemy aircraft. In July 1940 she was damaged by aircraft off Portland but was soon repaired and at sea again. On 5th November 1940 the German battleship ADMIRAL SCHEER attacked her convoy and sank the merchant cruiser JERVIS BAY and six merchant ships but the BRIARWOOD survived. She was commodore ship of a North Russian convoy in May 1942 when an attack by five German destroyers and numerous aircraft was successfully held off. The cruiser H.M.S. EDINBURGH was sunk and the escorting destroyers suffered heavy casualties but again the BRIARWOOD arrived safely.

In 1945 only the BRIARWOOD and WEARWOOD remained of the deep-sea fleet together with five steamers of the coastal fleet and the motorships AVONWOOD and EDENWOOD which had been built during the war. The BRIARWOOD was sold to the Stag Line Ltd. of North Shields and the following year saw the sale of the WEARWOOD. The steamer EMPIRE BROMLEY was acquired and renamed LEVENWOOD, bringing the fleet to six steamers and two motorships. For some time the Company had been interested in entering the liner trade and in 1946 the opportunity was taken to acquire Whimster and Co. Ltd. of Glasgow. Prior to the war this company had been engaged in the Mediterranean trade with two steamers but both its vessels had been lost during the conflict. The motorship GARTWOOD was delivered for this service in 1946 and in 1949 the LOCHWOOD was completed for the same trade. The motorships AVONWOOD and EDENWOOD were fitted with 'tween decks and the accommodation was extended and modernised. The four ships, each with excellent passenger accommodation, maintained a regular service between Glasgow, Belfast, Dublin, Bristol Channel ports and Marseilles, Genoa, Leghorn, Naples and Sicily.

The Company expanded its shipbroking, forwarding and agency interests through Constantine and Co. (1947) Ltd. with branch offices at Southampton, Liverpool, Glasgow and Cardiff as well as in London. In later years branch offices were also located at Birmingham, London Airport, Southend Airport, Avonmouth and Harwich. In 1950 Neale and Wilkinson Ltd. was acquired together with its subsidiary companies, Stewart and Esplen Ltd. and the Sterling Wharfage Co. Ltd. who were engaged in shipping, forwarding, travel and wharfage.

The AVONWOOD and EDENWOOD commenced operations in Canada in 1953 and traded between Toronto, Hamilton, Montreal and St. John's, Newfoundland during the summer season, returning to the Mediterranean service in the winter months. In 1951 the motorships COPSEWOOD and ESKWOOD had been delivered and, with the TEESWOOD completed in 1953, they were employed in tramping between U.K. and Continental ports. Unfortunately the TEESWOOD was lost off Dungeness in July 1956 when she encountered a severe storm during a voyage from Blyth to Shoreham. In 1957 the TYNEWOOD and THAMESWOOD joined the fleet in the short-sea trade. They were raised quarter deck vessels capable of carrying many types of bulk cargo and had the machinery and accommodation situated aft. The rights of the Golden Cross Line Ltd. of Cardiff were acquired in 1959 and in the same year the Teesdale Steamship Co. Ltd. and the Tynedale Shipping Co. Ltd. were formed to own the newly acquired steamers HIGHLINER and YORKWOOD which were employed mainly in Canadian waters. As new tonnage had joined the fleet it was decided to dispose of the older steamers

CEDARWOOD   *E. N. Taylor*

which dated from the pre-war days together with the war-built motorships AVONWOOD and EDENWOOD. In October 1960 the EASTWOOD entered service but within the next decade the Company was to withdraw entirely from shipowning.

In 1963 Mr. R. A. Constantine retired as chairman of the Joseph Constantine Steamship Line Ltd. and he was succeeded by Mr. H. N. Constantine. In 1966 it was decided to wind up the Joseph Constantine Steamship Line Ltd. and for it to be replaced by a new parent company known as Constantine Holdings Ltd. As opportunities arose the sale of ships continued with the GARTWOOD in 1966, followed in 1967 by the COPSEWOOD, ESKWOOD, and TYNEWOOD. In 1968 the THAMESWOOD was sold and finally the EASTWOOD was handed over to Italian buyers. So ended eventful chapters in the history of the Constantine Companies.

Since 1968 the Companies have certainly progressed, considerable expansion having taken place in Freight Forwarding, Packing and Shipping Service activities, so that together they now form one of the most comprehensive Groups in the field within the U.K. At the same time on the Property side major expansion of the Group's various Real Estate interests have been achieved mainly in the U.K., Canada and the U.S.A.

These broadly based activities taken together now form a strong resilient platform on which further growth and development can be achieved. The Group may now be without the ships which formed its beginnings, but it can be said that it was in these beginnings that the successful enterprise which exists today has its foundations.

FLEET LIST NOTES

The notation '1', '2', etc., in brackets after a ship's name indicates that she is the first, second, etc., ship of that name in the fleet. The dates following the name are those of entering and leaving the fleet, or coming under and leaving the management of the Company.

On the first line is given the ship's Official Number (O.N.) in the British Registry, followed by her tonnages gross ('g') and net ('n'). Dimensions given are registered length x beam x depth in feet and tenths for ships numbered 1-83 and M1-M36 and the overall length x beam x draught at summer deadweight for the ships numbered 84-91.

On the second line is given the type of engines and the name of the engine builders 'C.2-cyl.' denotes compound two cylinder steam engines, 'T.3-cyl.' = triple expansion three cylinder steam engines, 'Q.4-cyl.' = quadruple expansion four cylinder steam engines and for motor vessels the number of cylinders is given and whether they are two stroke cycle (2 S.C.) or four stroke cycle (4 S.C.) single acting (S.A.).

The ships' histories are corrected up to February 1983.

HOMEWOOD   *Company Archives*

1. HOMEWOOD (1) (1885 — 1897)
1140g, 1065n, 180.0 x 36.5 x 22.8 feet
1874: Launched by Cruickshank and Pittfield, St. John N.B. for John F. Cruickshank, St. John
N.B. *1879:* Sold to Joseph G. Kenney, Liverpool. *1885:* Purchased by Actieselskabet Homewood
(Chr. Klaveness manager), Norway. *1897:* Sold to F. Melsom, Norway. *19.3.1903:* Wrecked near
Risor whilst on a voyage from Fredrikstad to Capetown.

NORWOOD   *Company Archives*

2. NORWOOD (1887 — 1896)
1657g, 1587n, 221.6 x 39.3 x 24.4 feet
1874: Launched by McFee, St. John N.B. as P. G. CARVILL for P. G. Carvill, Liverpool. *1887:*
Purchased by Actieselskabet Norwood (Chr. Klaveness manager), Norway and renamed
NORWOOD. *1896:* Sold to H. Fredriksen, Norway and renamed SOLHEIM. *27.2.1900:*
Abandoned in the North Atlantic whilst on a voyage from Mobile to Fleetwood with a cargo of
pitch pine.

3. TOFTWOOD (1) (1891 — 1902)
1060g, 687n, 220.5 × 30.1 × 16.6 feet
C. 2-cyl. by G. Clark, Sunderland.
7.1872: Launched by Robert Thompson Jnr., Sunderland as SANTORIN for Lumsdon, Byers and Co., Sunderland. *1882:* Sold to R. T. Nicholson, Sunderland. *1891:* Purchased by Actieselskabet Santorin (Chr. Klaveness manager), Norway and renamed TOFTWOOD. *1897:* Registered under Actieselskabet Toftwood (same manager), Norway. *1902:* Sold to A. J. Myhre, Norway and renamed CLARA. *1902:* Sold to Actieselskabet Clara (O. Mohn manager), Norway. *1904:* Renamed LINA. *2.5.1908:* Wrecked at Balanec, near Molene whilst on a voyage from Barry to Arcachon with a cargo of coal.

4. COPSEWOOD (1) (1892 — 1895)
1116g, 709n, 240.5 × 33.2 × 14.0 feet.
C. 2-cyl. by Hutson and Corbett, Glasgow.
8.1882: Launched by Dobson and Charles, Grangemouth as CRAIGHILL for Walker, Donald and Co., Glasgow. *1887:* Sold to W. Turner, Glasgow. *1889:* Sold to R. Mackill and Co., Glasgow. *1892:* Purchased by Actieselskabet Copsewood (Chr. Klaveness manager), Norway and renamed COPSEWOOD. *16.10.1895:* Wrecked near Cross Islands whilst on a voyage from Archangel to London with a cargo of wood.

WESTWOOD at Truro in 1893

Brownell Collection

5. WESTWOOD (1)/TEESWOOD (2) (1892 — 1914)
ON. 86492, 1641g, 1018n, 278.5 × 36.1 × 18.5 feet.
C. 2-cyl. by J. Dickinson, Sunderland.
10.1882: Launched by Short Bros., Sunderland as BRITANNIA for United Kingdom S.S. Co. Ltd. (Short and Dunn managers), Cardiff having been laid down for Sunderland S.S. Co. Ltd. (Peckett, Thompson and Co. managers), Sunderland. *1890:* Management transferred to Cory Bros. and Co., Cardiff. *1892:* Purchased by Actieselskabet Westwood (Chr. Klaveness manager), Norway and renamed WESTWOOD. *1907:* Management transferred to W. Holby, Norway. *1913:* Transferred to Constantine and Pickering S.S. Co. Ltd., registered under the British flag and renamed TEESWOOD. *1914:* Sold to The Admiralty and scuttled as a blockship at Scapa Flow.

6. LINWOOD (1) (1894 — 1916)
ON. 101921. 1660g, 1056n, 250.0 × 35.2 × 16.6 feet.
T. 3-cyl. by G. Clark Ltd., Sunderland.
9.1892: Completed by Blyth Shipbuilding Co. Ltd., Blyth as GONDOLA for Gondola S.S. Co. Ltd. (W. Lamplough and Co. managers), London. *1894:* Purchased by Actieselskabet Linwood (Chr. Klaveness manager), Norway and renamed LINWOOD. *1907:* Transferred to Constantine and Pickering S.S. Co. and registered under the British flag. *1916:* Sold to Valcares Co. Ltd. (H. Johnson, Sons and Co. Ltd. managers), London. *22.1.1917:* Sailed from Gibraltar whilst on a voyage from Carthagena to Maryport with a cargo of iron ore and disappeared.

7. HELMSWOOD (1895 — 1899)
1860g, 1194n, 265.1 x 36.0 x 19.7 feet.
C. 2-cyl. by Blair and Co. Ltd., Stockton on Tees.
3.1883: Launched by Wm. Gray and Co., West Hartlepool as HELMSLEY for Hudson Shipping Co. Ltd., West Hartlepool. *1895:* Purchased by Actieselskabet Helmswood (Chr. Klaveness manager), Norway and renamed HELMSWOOD. *1899:* Sold to Rederiaktieb. Orlando (J. A. Enhorning manager), Sweden and renamed ORLANDO. *1903:* Management transferred to E. A. Enhorning. *1935:* Sold to shipbreakers.

8. LAURELWOOD (1896 — 1904)
ON. 109233. 2845g, 1595n, 290.0 x 43.0 x 16.5 feet.
T. 3-cyl. by Blair and Co. Ltd., Stockton on Tees.
4.1896: Completed by Ropner and Son, Stockton on Tees for Actieselskabet Laurelwood (Chr. Klaveness manager), Norway. *1897:* Transferred to Constantine, Pickering and Co. and registered under the British flag. *1901:* Transferred to Constantine and Pickering S.S. Co. *11.1.1904:* Wrecked at Chausse de Sein, France whilst on a voyage from Rio de Janeiro to Middlesbrough with a cargo of manganese ore.

KINGSWOOD *G. Scott Collection*

9. KINGSWOOD (1) (1896 — 1916)
ON. 119805. 1907g, 1209n, 270.0 x 39.5 x 14.4 feet.
T. 3-cyl. by Blair and Co. Ltd., Stockton on Tees.
6.1896: Completed by Ropner and Son, Stockton on Tees for Actieselskabet Kingswood (Chr. Klaveness manager), Norway. *1907:* Transferred to Constantine and Pickering S.S. Co. and registered under the British flag. *1916:* Sold to Bolivian General Enterprise Ltd. (Leopold Walford (London) Ltd. managers), London. *15.3.1917:* Sank 8 miles W. of Ile de Groix following a collision with the French steamer CORNEILLE, 2233/89 whilst on a voyage from R. Tyne to Bayonne with a cargo of coal.

10. RIFTSWOOD (1897 — 1907)
ON. 98148. 1832g, 1166n, 260.0 x 36.6 x 16.6 feet
T. 3-cyl. by Westgarth, English and Co., Middlesbrough.
8.1890: Completed by R. Craggs and Sons, Middlesbrough as SAM HANDFORD for G. Page, London. *1896:* Sold to J. Holman and Sons, London. *1897:* Purchased by Constantine, Pickering and Co. and renamed RIFTSWOOD. *1901:* Transferred to Constantine and Pickering S.S. Co. *5.3.1907:* Abandoned on fire S.E. of North Point, St. Lucia whilst on a voyage from Cardiff to Barbados and Dominica with a cargo of coal.

11. QUEENSWOOD (1) (1897 — 1917)
ON. 98790. 2701g, 1694n, 300.0 x 45.0 x 20.4 feet.
T. 3-cyl. by Blair and Co. Ltd., Stockton on Tees.
9.1897: Completed by Ropner and Son, Stockton on Tees for Constantine, Pickering and Co. *1901:* Transferred to Constantine and Pickering S.S. Co. *16.2.1917:* Sunk by gunfire 6 miles S. W. of Hartland Point after being attacked by the German submarine UC.65 whilst on a voyage from Rouen to Port Talbot in ballast.

12. HOMEWOOD (2) (1897 — 1916)

ON. 109231. 2024g, 1291n, 271.0 × 40.5 × 17.4 feet
T. 3-cyl. by Sir C. Furness, Westgarth and Co. Ltd., Middlesbrough.
12.1897: Completed by R. Craggs and Sons, Middlesbrough for Constantine, Pickering and Co.
1901: Transferred to Constantine and Pickering S.S. Co. *1916:* Sold to Aldershot S.S. Co. Ltd.
(W. Fletcher and Son Ltd. managers), London and renamed SILSDEN *1919:* Sold to Alfred
Calvert (Shipping) Ltd. (A. Calvert manager), Goole and renamed ERIC CALVERT. *1923:* Sold to
Calvert S.S. Co. Ltd. (J. S. Calvert manager), Goole. *1927:* Sold to L. Baltas (P.P. Lascarides
manager), Greece and renamed DOROTHEA, *1931:* Sold to X. Siderides, Greece and renamed
FLORENTIA S. *1934:* Sold to E. N. Vintiadis, Greece and renamed GIORGAKIS, *1935:* Sold to
Giuseppe Palomba fu Michele, Italy and renamed PEPPINO PALOMBA. *8.5.1943:* Torpedoed
and sunk near Santa Maura Island, Greece by the British submarine H.M.S. SAFARI.

EARLSWOOD   *J. Clarkson*

13. EARLSWOOD (1898 — 1916)

ON. 109234. 2353g, 1480n, 300.0 × 43.0 × 20.4 feet.
T. 3-cyl. by Sir C. Furness, Westgarth and Co. Ltd., Middlesbrough.
10.1898: Completed by R. Craggs and Sons, Middlesbrough for Constantine, Pickering and Co.
1901: Transferred to Constantine and Pickering S.S. Co. *1916:* Sold to Federated Coal and
Shipping Co. Ltd., Cardiff. *1919:* Sold to Aster Shipping Co. Ltd. (E. R. Brown manager), Cardiff.
1923: Sold to A.F.M. Dacker (J. Cormack and Co. managers), Leith and renamed DARIUS. *1923:*
Sold to W. Schuchmann, Germany and renamed WESTSEE. *1926:* Sold to Robert Koppen,
Germany and renamed ELSA KOPPEN. *1932:* Sold to W. Schuchmann, Germany and renamed
LUVSEE: *23.9.1941:* Torpedoed and sunk off Sibenik by the British submarine H.M.S. TRIUMPH.

14. ROSEWOOD (1899 — 1914)

ON. 88817. 1757g, 1104n, 259.0 × 36.0 × 17.9 feet.
T. 3-cyl. by the Shipbuilders.
1.1889: Completed by J. Readhead and Sons, South Shields as BLAKEMOOR for W. Runciman
and Co., South Shields. *1897:* Registered under North Moor Steamships Ltd. (W. Runciman and
Co. managers), Newcastle upon Tyne. *1899:* Purchased by W. Constantine and renamed
ROSEWOOD. *1901:* Transferred to Constantine and Pickering S.S. Co. *1914:* Sold to The
Admiralty and scuttled as a blockship at Scapa Flow.

15. LOCHWOOD (1) (1900 — 1915)

ON. 109237. 2042g, 1310n, 289.0 × 43.3 × 20.0 feet.
T. 3-cyl. by North Eastern Marine Engineering Co. Ltd., Sunderland.
2.1900: Completed by Craig, Taylor and Co., Stockton on Tees for Constantine, Pickering and
Co. *1901:* Transferred to Constantine and Pickering S.S. Co. *2.4.1915:* Torpedoed and sunk 25
miles S. W. of Start Point by the German submarine U.24 whilst on a voyage from Barry with
a cargo of coal.

LOCHWOOD   *World Ship Photo Library*

16. GOODWOOD (1) (1900 — 1917)
ON. 109239. 3086g, 1977n, 325.0 × 48.1 × 21.9 feet.
T. 3-cyl. by Blair and Co. Ltd., Stockton on Tees.
9.1900: Completed by Ropner and Son, Stockton on Tees for Constantine, Pickering and Co.
1901: Transferred to Constantine and Pickering S.S. Co. *1917:* Transferred to Joseph
Constantine. *21.8.1917:* Torpedoed and sunk 28 miles N.W. by N. from Cape Bon by the
German submarine UC.67 whilst on a voyage from Naples to Tunis in ballast.

HAZELWOOD   *World Ship Photo Library*

17. HAZELWOOD (1) (1904 — 1916)
ON. 113908. 3102g, 1992n, 325.0 × 48.0 × 23.1 feet.
T. 3-cyl. by Blair and Co. Ltd., Stockton on Tees.
2.1904: Completed by Ropner and Son, Stockton on Tees for Constantine and Pickering S.S. Co.
1916: Sold to Gascony Shipping Co. Ltd. (Leopold Walford (London) Ltd. managers), London.
18.10.1917: Mined and sunk 8 miles S. by E.$\frac{1}{2}$E. from Anvil Point.

BROOKWOOD
H. S. Appleyard Collection

18. BROOKWOOD (1) (1904 — 1917)
ON. 113909. 3093g, 1987n, 325.0 × 48.0 × 23.2 feet.
T. 3-cyl. by Blair and Co. Ltd., Stockton on Tees.
3.1904: Completed by Ropner and Son, Stockton on Tees for Constantine and Pickering S.S. Co.
1907: Transferred to Constantine, Pickering and Co. *10.1.1917:* Sunk by gunfire 210 miles N.
by W. from Cape Finisterre after being attacked by the German submarine U.79 whilst on a
voyage from Penarth to Port Said with a cargo of coal.

KIRNWOOD
H. S. Appleyard Collection

19. KIRNWOOD (1) (1905 — 1922)
ON. 113910. 3049g, 1953n, 330.1 × 47.0 × 22.2 feet.
T. 3-cyl. by Blair and Co. Ltd., Stockton on Tees.
7.1905: Completed by R. Craggs and Sons Ltd., Middlesbrough for Constantine and Pickering
S.S. Co. *1917:* Transferred to Joseph Constantine. *1921:* Transferred to Wood Line Ltd. *1922:*
Sold to D. M. Logothetis, Greece and renamed MICHAEL. *1933:* Sold to A. Vlassov and P.
Argyropoulos (C. Arvanitides manager), Greece and renamed MIMOSA. *1935:* Sold to Societe
Commerciale et d'Armement Soc. Anon., Greece. *1948:* Sold to Cia. Argentina de Nav. de
Ultramar S.A., Panama. *1950:* Sold to Giuseppe Ricardi and broken up by Maria Bertorello who
commenced demolition on *22.5.1950* at Vado.

20. HUTTONWOOD (1905 — 1919)
ON. 119801. 3903g, 2533n, 340.2 × 47.2 × 20.0 feet.
T. 3-cyl. by Blair and Co. Ltd., Stockton on Tees.
10.1905: Completed by R. Stephenson and Co. Ltd., Newcastle upon Tyne for Constantine and Pickering S.S. Co. *1917:* Transferred to Joseph Constantine. *1919:* Sold to A/S. D/S. Henrik Lund (W.C. Gilbert manager), Norway and renamed HENRIK LUND. *1924:* Sold to D/S. Ulvo A/S. (H. Ostervold manager), Norway and renamed ULVO. *1929:* Sold to Skibs A/S. Thetis (J. W. Prebensen manager), Norway and renamed THETIS. *1931:* Sold to D/S. Eidsvold A/S. (H. Ostervold manager), Norway. *1933:* Sold to Metal Industries Ltd. and broken up at Rosyth.

21. PARKWOOD (1) (1906 — 1915)
ON. 119803. 1779g, 1102n, 272.5 × 40.2 × 18.1 feet.
T. 3-cyl. by Richardsons, Westgarth and Co. Ltd., Middlesbrough.
5.1906: Completed by Sir Raylton Dixon and Co. Ltd., Middlesbrough for Constantine and Pickering S.S. Co. *14.7.1915:* Wrecked in the White Sea, in a position 67.10N. 42.53E., whilst on a voyage from Blyth to Archangel with a cargo of coal.

22. TOFTWOOD (2) (1906 — 1917)
ON. 119806. 3082g, 1961n, 330.1 × 47.0 × 22.2 feet.
T. 3-cyl. by Blair and Co. Ltd., Stockton on Tees.
10.1906: Completed by R. Craggs and Sons Ltd., Middlesbrough for Constantine and Pickering S. S. Co. *13.1.1917:* Torpedoed and sunk 24 miles N.$\frac{1}{2}$W from Sept Isles by the German submarine UC.18 whilst on a voyage from New York to Le Havre with general cargo.

HARLSEYWOOD

E. Johnson

23. HARLSEYWOOD (1907 — 1923)
ON. 125142. 2701g, 1694n, 317.0 × 46.0 × 20.9 feet.
T. 3-cyl. by Blair and Co. Ltd., Stockton on Tees.
12.1907: Completed by Ropner and Sons Ltd., Stockton on Tees for Constantine and Pickering S. S. Co. *1917:* Transferred to Joseph Constantine. *1921:* Transferred to Joseph Constantine S.S. Line Ltd. *1921:* Transferred to Wood Line Ltd. *1923:* Sold to Rederiakt. Protector (Olson and Wright managers), Sweden and renamed WRIGHT. *1929:* Sold to Limhamns Rederi A/B. (Edv. Persson manager), Sweden and renamed ESKIL. *1939:* Sold to Rederi A/B. Rex (K. M. Kallstrom manager), Sweden and renamed NAMDO. *12.8.1944:* Mined and sunk in R. Elbe whilst on a voyage from Lulea to Bremen with a cargo of iron ore. *20.10.1944:* Raised but broke in two and sank.

CEDARWOOD   *E. N. Taylor*

24. CEDARWOOD (1) (1907 — 1916)
ON. 125143. 654g, 257n, 176.0 × 29.8 × 10.8 feet.
T. 3-cyl. by Blair and Co. Ltd., Stockton on Tees.
12.1907: Completed by W. Harkess and Son Ltd., Middlesbrough for Meteor S.S. Co. Ltd.
12.2.1916: Mined and sunk 2½ miles from Aldborough Napes whilst on a voyage from
Middlesbrough to Fecamp with a cargo of pig iron.

LINDENHALL   *J. Howden*

25. LINDENHALL (1908 — 1912)
ON. 112421. 4003g, 2595n, 345.0 × 47.9 × 19.4 feet.
T. 3-cyl. by Sir C. Furness, Westgarth and Co. Ltd., Middlesbrough.
9.1900: Completed by Irvine's S.B. and D.D. Co. Ltd., West Hartlepool as LINDENHALL for The
West Hartlepool S.N. Co. Ltd., West Hartlepool. *1908:* Purchased by Constantine and Pickering
S.S. Co. *1912:* Sold to The West Hartlepool S.N. Co. Ltd., West Hartlepool. *1924:* Sold to
Societa Anonima per l'Industria ed il Commercio Marittimo Nova Genuensis, Italy and renamed
HUMILITAS. *1926:* Sold to Societa Anonima Industria Armamento, Italy. *30.1.1929:* Wrecked
at Aksas whilst on a voyage from Reggio to Black Sea in ballast.

26. PURITAN (1908 — 1914)
ON. 106875. 4042g, 2553n, 356.0 × 45.2 × 20.0 feet.
T. 3-cyl. by W. Allan and Co. Ltd., Sunderland.
9.1897: Completed by Craig, Taylor and Co., Stockton on Tees as PURITAN for Puritan S.S. Co.
Ltd. (R. Stewart and Co. managers), Liverpool. *1905:* Managers restyled as Papayanni and
Stewart. *1906:* Managers restyled as Stewart and Tyrer. *1908:* Purchased by Constantine and
Pickering S.S. Co. *1914:* Sold to Goshi Kaisha Tatsuuma Shokai, Japan and renamed KEISHIN
MARU. *1923:* Sold to Kita Shina Kisen K. K. (North China S.S. Co. Ltd.) (Mikami and Co. Ltd.
managers), Japan. *1931:* Sold to shipbreakers.

PURITAN   *World Ship Photo Library*

27. COPSEWOOD (2) (1908 — 1916)
ON. 125145. 599g, 352n, 176.0 × 29.8 × 10.6 feet.
T. 3-cyl. by MacColl and Pollock Ltd., Sunderland.
9.1908: Completed by R. Thompson and Sons Ltd., Sunderland for Meteor S.S. Co. Ltd.
27.12.1916: Torpedoed and sunk 34 miles S. by W. $\frac{3}{4}$W. from the Lizard by the German submarine U.79 whilst on a voyage from Bordeaux to Middlesbrough with a cargo of pitwood.

28. LARCHWOOD (1) (1910 — 1916)
ON. 128803. 689g, 291n, 180.0 × 29.8 × 10.9 feet.
T. 3-cyl. by Blair and Co. Ltd., Stockton on Tees.
2.1910: Completed by W. Harkess and Son Ltd., Middlesbrough for Meteor S.S. Co. Ltd.
14.1.1916: Sank 3 miles S. by E. from Bull Point following a collision with the British steamer ARGUS, 1238/83 whilst on a voyage from Penarth with a cargo of coal.

BIRCHWOOD at Port St. Joe, Florida   *H. S. Appleyard Collection*

29. BIRCHWOOD (1910 — 1918)
ON. 128804. 2756g, 1780n, 317.0 × 45.8 × 22.1 feet.
T. 3-cyl by Blair and Co. Ltd., Stockton on Tees.
3.1910: Completed by Ropner and Sons Ltd., Stockton on Tees for Birchwood S.S. Co. Ltd.
3.1.1918: Torpedoed and sunk 25 miles E. of the Blackwater Light Vessel by the German submarine U.61 whilst on a voyage from R. Clyde to Devonport with a cargo of coal.

30. MORDENWOOD (1910 — 1917)
ON. 128808. 3125g, 1977n, 331.0 × 47.0 × 23.3 feet.
T. 3-cyl. by Blair and Co. Ltd., Stockton on Tees.
6.1910: Completed by Ropner and Sons Ltd., Stockton on Tees for Constantine and Pickering S.S. Co. *1917:* Transferred to Joseph Constantine. *19.5.1917:* Torpedoed and sunk by the Austrian submarine U.XXIX 90 miles S.E. by S$\frac{1}{2}$S from Cape Matapan.

31. TEESWOOD (1) (1910 — 1911)
ON. 128809. 407g, 197n, 145.0 × 24.1 × 10.4 feet.
C. 2-cyl. by Richardsons, Westgarth and Co. Ltd., Middlesbrough.
7.1910: Completed by W. Harkess and Son Ltd., Middlesbrough for Meteor S. S. Co. Ltd. *1911:* Sold to Sydney Coal Co. Ltd., Sydney, N.S.W. *1912:* Renamed YULOO. *1921:* Sold to Australian Steamships Pty. Ltd. (Howard Smith Ltd. manager), Melbourne. *1929:* Sold to H. P. Stacey, Sydney N.S.W. *1932:* Sold to shipbreakers.

32. LEVENWOOD (1) (1911 — 1915)
ON. 128812. 791g, 370n, 195.0 × 30.0 × 11.6 feet.
T. 3-cyl. by Blair and Co. Ltd., Stockton on Tees.
7.1911: Completed by W. Harkess and Son Ltd., Middlesbrough for Meteor S.S. Co. Ltd. *1915:* Sold to Plymouth Mutual Co-operative and Industrial Society Ltd. (E.E. Wonnacott manager), Plymouth and renamed CHARLES GOODANEW. *17.4.1917:* Mined and sunk 3$\frac{1}{2}$ miles E.N.E. of Rattray Head.

ESKWOOD   *Brownell Collection*

33. ESKWOOD (1) (1911 — 1918)
ON. 128813. 791g, 370n, 195.0 × 30.0 × 11.6 feet.
T. 3-cyl. by Blair and Co. Ltd., Stockton on Tees.
8.1911: Completed by W. Harkess and Son Ltd., Middlesbrough for Meteor S.S. Co. Ltd. *1918:* Sold to E. Johnson and Co. Ltd., Goole. *1926:* Sold to S. & R. Steamships Ltd. (Stone and Rolfe Ltd. managers), Llanelly, *1937:* Sold to Mersey Ports Stevedoring Co. Ltd., Liverpool. *1943:* Sold to Grand Union (Shipping) Ltd., London. *1946:* Renamed KILWORTH. *1950:* Sold to Fenchurch Shipping Co. Ltd. (Geo. A. Tom and Co. Ltd. managers), London and renamed FENCHURCH. *1951:* Sold to Holderness S.S. Co. Ltd., Hull and renamed HOLDERNOLL. *1956:* Sold to British Iron and Steel Corporation, allocated to J. J. King and Co. Ltd. and arrived at Gateshead *20.1.1956* to be broken up.

THORPWOOD *Brownell Collection*

34. THORPWOOD (1912 — 1915)
ON. 128815. 3184g, 1980n, 335.0 × 48.0 × 23.4 feet.
T. 3-cyl. by Central Marine Engine Works, West Hartlepool.
3.1912: Completed by Wm. Gray and Co. Ltd., West Hartlepool for Constantine and Pickering S. S. Co. Ltd., *8.10.1915:* Sunk by gunfire 122 miles S. of Cape Martello, Crete after being attacked by the German submarine U.39 whilst on a voyage from R. Tyne via Malta with a cargo of coal.

WEARWOOD *A. Duncan*

35. WEARWOOD (1) (1912 — 1926)
ON. 128817. 3221g, 2013n, 335.0 × 48.0 × 22.4 feet.
T. 3-cyl. by North Eastern Marine Engineering Co. Ltd., Sunderland.
5.1912: Completed by J. Blumer and Co., Sunderland for Constantine and Pickering S.S. Co. Ltd. *1917:* Transferred to Joseph Constantine. *1921:* Transferred to Joseph Constantine S.S. Line Ltd. *1926:* Sold to Dairen Kisen K.K., Japan and renamed ROKO MARU. *11.8.1944:* Torpedoed and sunk by the U.S. submarine TANG S.W. of Nagoya, in a position 34.12N. 136.19E.

36. TRENTWOOD (1912 — 1923)
ON. 128818. 791g, 369n, 195.0 × 30.0 × 11.7 feet.
T. 3-cyl. by Blair and Co. Ltd., Stockton on Tees.
6.1912: Completed by W. Harkess and Son Ltd., Middlesbrough for Meteor S.S. Co. Ltd. *1918:* Transferred to R. A. Constantine and T. H. Donking. *1920:* Transferred to Constantine and Donking S.S. Co. Ltd. *1923:* Sold to Donking S.S. Co. Ltd. (T.H. Donking manager), Middlesbrough. *1925:* Managers restyled as T.H. Donking and Sons Ltd. *1953:* Sold to British Iron and Steel Corporation, allocated to C. W. Dorkin and Co. and broken up at Redheugh on Tyne.

37. WARLEY PICKERING (1912 — 1917)

ON. 128819. 4196g, 2647n, 365.0 × 51.2 × 26.1 feet.
T. 3-cyl. by Blair and Co. Ltd., Stockton on Tees.
8.1912: Completed by Sir Raylton Dixon and Co. Ltd., Middlesbrough for Constantine and Pickering S.S. Co. Ltd. *5.2.1917:* Torpedoed and sunk 46 miles W. by N. from Fastnet by the German submarine U.60 whilst on a voyage from Sagunto to Middlesbrough with a cargo of iron ore.

38. TAYWOOD (1915 — 1922)

ON. 98784. 491g, 161n, 155.0 × 26.8 × 11.7 feet.
T. 3-cyl. by J. Dickinson and Sons, Sunderland. Replaced in 1946 by a 8-cyl. 4 S.C.S.A. oil engine by Klockner-Humboldt-Deutz A. G., Cologne.
4.1894: Completed by J. L. Thompson and Sons, Sunderland as CATTERSTY for Skinningrove Iron Co. Ltd. (T.C. Hutchinson manager), Middlesbrough. *1915:* Purchased by R. A. Constantine and T. H. Donking and renamed TAYWOOD. *1920:* Transferred to Constantine and Donking S.S. Co. Ltd. *1922:* Sold to J. Geddes, Yarmouth. *1923:* Placed under the management of Robinson, Brown and Co., Newcastle upon Tyne and renamed GLEDHILL. *1927:* Sold to H. Sergo, Estonia and renamed VALVE. *1930:* Sold to Puutoostusuhisus "Esthag", Estonia. *1933:* Sold to M. and A. Utow, Estonia. *1934:* Sold to H. Roman, Estonia and renamed HILDA. *1938:* Sold to M. Utow, Estonia and renamed HILDE. *1945:* Sold to Rederi A/B. Ponape (G. Erikson manager), Finland and renamed STYRSO. *1949:* Registered under Rederi A/B, Styrso (F: a Gustaf Erikson manager). *1954:* Registered under Mariehamns Rederi A/B. (same managers) *1959:* Sold to Rederibolaget Adina (Waldemar Hoglund manager), Finland and renamed ADINA. *1967:* Sold to Bengt Birger Lindroos, Finland. *1968:* Sold to Rederibolaget Sonja (Peter Kalley manager), Finland and renamed SONJA. *1970:* Sold to Personer A/B and broken up at Ystad.

39. ELLAWOOD (1915 — 1918)

ON. 136072. 3100g, 1911n, 335.5 × 48.1 × 23.3 feet.
T. 3-cyl. by Blair and Co. Ltd., Stockton on Tees.
4.1915: Completed by Ropner and Sons Ltd., Stockton on Tees for Constantine and Pickering S.S. Co. Ltd. *1917:* Transferred to Joseph Constantine. *1918:* Sold to A. C. Ioannou, London. *1919:* Sold to J. McKelvie, London. *1920:* Renamed NELDA. *1921:* Sold to A. and C. Aboaf Ltd., London. *1922:* Sold to Soc. Geral de Commercio Industria e Transportes Ltda., Portugal and renamed PINHEL. *1950:* Sold to British Iron and Steel Corporation, allocated to P. and W. McLellan Ltd. and broken up at Bo'ness. *2.7.1950:* Sailed from Lisbon as BISCO 2 bound for Bo'ness.

40. BILSWOOD (1915 — 1917)

ON. 136073. 3097g, 1911n, 335.1 × 48.0 × 23.3 feet.
T. 3-cyl. by Blair and Co. Ltd., Stockton on Tees.
6.1915: Completed by Ropner and Sons Ltd., Stockton on Tees for Joseph Constantine. *12.3.1917:* Mined and sunk 8 miles N.W. of Alexandria whilst on a voyage from Malta.

TEESWOOD *World Ship Photo Library*

41. TEESWOOD (3) (1915 — 1917)
ON. 136075. 864g, 416n, 198.0 × 30.6 × 12.5 feet.
T. 3-cyl. by Blair and Co. Ltd., Stockton on Tees.
7.1915: Completed by W. Harkess and Son Ltd., Middlesbrough for R.A. Constantine and T. H. Donking. *1917:* Sold to Commercial Gas Co., London. *1924:* Sold to Donking S.S. Co. Ltd. (T. H. Donking manager), Middlesbrough. *1925:* Managers restyled as T. H. Donking and Sons Ltd. *28.11.1951:* Wrecked on Borkum Island whilst on a voyage from Immingham to Emden with a cargo of slag.

EDENWOOD as **EDEN FORCE**   *E. N. Taylor*

42. EDENWOOD (1) (1915 — 1918)
ON. 136076. 863g, 414n, 198.0 × 30.7 × 12.4 feet.
T. 3-cyl. by Blair and Co. Ltd., Stockton on Tees.
8.1915: Completed by Ropner and Sons Ltd., Stockton on Tees for R. A. Constantine and T. H. Donking. *1918:* Transferred to Meteor S.S. Co. Ltd. *1918:* Sold to West Coast Shipping Co. Ltd. (W.S. Kennaugh and Co. managers), Liverpool and renamed EDEN FORCE. *10.12.1940:* Sank whilst at anchor in Barry Roads following a collision with the British steamer NICETO DE LARRINAGA, 5591/16 whilst on a voyage from Liverpool to Bristol with a cargo of copra.

MAPLEWOOD   *E. Johnson*

43. MAPLEWOOD (1) (1915 — 1917)
ON. 136078. 3239g, 2017n, 335.0 × 48.1 × 23.4 feet.
T. 3-cyl. by Blair and Co. Ltd., Stockton on Tees.
10.1915: Completed by Ropner and Sons Ltd., Stockton on Tees for Constantine and Pickering S.S. Co. Ltd. *7.4.1917:* Torpedoed and sunk 47 miles S.W. of Cape Sperone, Sardinia by the German submarine U.35 whilst on a voyage from La Goulette to West Hartlepool.

AVONWOOD as BROOMFLEET   *E. N. Taylor*

44. AVONWOOD (1) (1915 — 1917)
ON. 136080. 864g, 414n, 198.1 x 30.7 x 12.4 feet.
T. 3-cyl. by MacColl and Pollock Ltd., Sunderland.
11.1915: Completed by W. Harkess and Son Ltd., Middlesbrough for R.A. Constantine and T. H. Donking. *1917:* Sold to London Transport Co. Ltd. (Brown, Jenkinson and Co. managers), London. *1919:* Sold to H. Rees Jones and Co. Ltd., Cardiff. *1920:* Sold to Wandsworth, Wimbledon and Epsom District Gas Co., London. *1924:* Sold to Ebor S.S. Co. Ltd. (A.W. Atkinson manager), Goole and renamed BROOMFLEET. *13.12.1933:* Sailed from Goole on a voyage to Ipswich with a cargo of coal and disappeared. Presumed to have foundered off Sheringham the same day.

ETHELWYNNE   *World Ship Photo Library*

45. ETHELWYNNE (1919 — 1920)
ON. 118851. 3230g, 2067n, 332.1 x 46.6 x 22.0 feet.
T. 3-cyl. by the Shipbuilders.
1904: Completed by Wm. Doxford and Sons Ltd., Sunderland as ETHELWYNNE for J. H. Harrowing. Whitby after being launched as ANDROS for Dryden S.S.Co. Ltd., London. *1905:* Sold to Robert Harrowing and Co., Whitby. *1908:* Sold to Harrowing S.S. Co. Ltd. (R. Harrowing and Co. managers), Whitby. *1919:* Purchased by Joseph Constantine. *1920:* Transferred to Joseph Constantine S.S. Line Ltd. *1920:* Sold to The New Steam Navigation and Trading Co. Ltd., Bombay. *1922:* Sold to Shinsei Kisen Goshi Kaisha, Japan and renamed SHINSEI MARU No. 6. *16.3.1931:* Wrecked at Hainan Bluff whilst on a voyage from Hongay to Hong Kong.

46. BRIARWOOD (1) (1919 — 1921)

ON. 142762. 5263g, 3198n, 400.0 × 52.4 × 28.4 feet.
T. 3-cyl. by Blair and Co. Ltd., Stockton on Tees.
1919: Completed by Ropner and Sons Ltd., Stockton on Tees as WAR MALLOW for The Shipping Controller (Stamp, Mann and Co. managers). *1919:* Purchased by Joseph Constantine and renamed BRIARWOOD. *1921:* Sold to Woodfield Steam Shipping Co. Ltd. (Woods, Tylor and Brown managers), London and renamed HEATHFIELD. *1933:* Sold to A.D. Callinicos, Greece and renamed NEDON. *1938:* Sold to Hugo Trumpy, Italy and renamed FAUSTO. *1942:* Seized at Montevideo by the Uruguayan Government and renamed MALDONALDO. *2.8.1942:* Torpedoed and sunk by the German submarine U.510 in a position 28.20N. 63.10W.

COYTOBEE   *Tees Pilotage Authority*

47. COYTOBEE (1920 — 1923)

ON. 114843. 156g, 100.0 × 18.6 × 9.7 feet.
C. 2-cyl. by the Shipbuilders.
1902: Completed by J. P. Rennoldson and Sons Ltd., South Shields as MARETANZA for Sir John Denison-Pender, London. *1902:* Sold to George H. Strutt (John Monro manager), Kingairloch and renamed SANDA. *1912:* Sold to Walter S. Jones, London and renamed COYTOBEE. *1916:* Sold to Joseph Constant, London. *1918:* Sold to Martin Constant, London. *1920:* Sold to Tees Pilotage Commissioners, Middlesbrough. *1920:* Purchased by Joseph Constantine. *1923:* Sold to Tees Pilot Cutter Co. Ltd., Middlesbrough. *1933:* Sold to shipbreakers.

48. POLMINA (1920 — 1922)

ON. 140434. 870g, 409n, 200.9 × 30.1 × 12.5 feet.
T. 3-cyl. by the Shipbuilders.
2.1917: Completed by Verschure and Co's Scheepswerf en Machinefabriek, Amsterdam as HERMINA for Nederlandsche Vrachtvaart Maatschappij, Holland. *10.9.1917:* Captured by a British warship in the North Sea, allocated to The Shipping Controller (Coast Lines Ltd. managers) and renamed POLMINA. *1920:* Purchased by Constantine and Donking S.S. Co. Ltd. *1922:* Sold to Haig Shipping Co. Ltd. (King and Co. (Cardiff) Ltd. managers), Cardiff. *1926:* Sold to R. Nilsson, Germany and renamed OSKAR. *1932:* Renamed ELSA MARIE. *1934:* Sold to E. Wietendorf (Carl Boch and Co. G.m.b.H. managers), Germany and renamed ELSA. *1.12.1936:* Foundered off Borkum whilst on a voyage from Danzig to Cherbourg with a cargo of coal.

49. MADAME DORETTA (1921— 1923).

ON. 139077. 794g, 363n, 186.3 × 29.4 × 12.4 feet.
T. 3-cyl. by Richardsons, Westgarth and Co. Ltd., Middlesbrough.
8.1915: Completed by R. Williamson and Son, Workington as FRESHET for E. H. Sollas, London. *1917:* Sold to T. G. Beatley and Son, London and renamed DORETTA. *1920:* Renamed MADAME DORETTA. *1921:* Purchased by Constantine and Donking S.S. Co. Ltd. *1923:* Sold to West Yorkshire Steam Shipping Co. Ltd. (H. S. Greenacre manager), Goole, *1931:* Sold to A. F. Henry and McGregor Ltd., Leith and renamed DUNVEGAN HEAD. *1936:* Sold to Woodtown Shipping Co. Ltd. (Comben, Longstaff and Co. Ltd. managers), London and renamed WOODTOWN. *15.11.1939:* Mined and sunk $\frac{3}{4}$ mile N.E. of Spit Buoy near Margate.

50. ARDSHEAN/EDENWOOD (2) (1921 — 1930)

ON. 144784. 804g, 378n, 186.5 x 29.4 x 12.4 feet.
T. 3-cyl. by McKie and Baxter Ltd., Glasgow.
10.1920: Completed by R. Williamson and Son, Workington as ARDSHEAN for Adam Bros. Ltd.,
Aberdeen. *1921:* Purchased by Constantine and Donking S.S. Co. Ltd. *1922:* Transferred to
Joseph Constantine S. S. Line Ltd. *1924:* Renamed EDENWOOD. *1930:* Sold to Brunswick S.S.
Co. Ltd. (Pollexfen and Co. Ltd. managers), Liverpool and renamed POLGRANGE. *25.7.1940:*
Bombed and sunk off Dover.

51. MAPLEWOOD (2) (1922 — 1929)

ON. 144593. 3194g, 1987n, 342.2 x 48.0 x 21.9 feet.
T. 3-cyl. by J. Dickinson and Sons Ltd., Sunderland.
6.1920: Completed by R. Thompson and Sons Ltd., Sunderland as RONALEE for Universal S.N.
Co. Ltd. (P. Samuel and Co. Ltd. managers), London. *1922:* Purchased by Wood Line Ltd. *1922:*
Transferred to Joseph Constantine S.S. Line Ltd. and renamed MAPLEWOOD. *1929:* Sold to
Samuelsen and Olsens Rederi (Jens Samuelsen manager), Norway and renamed NOVASLI.
1935: Sold to Skibs A/S Novasli (same manager). *2.3.1945:* Torpedoed and sunk in the Irish Sea
by the German submarine U.1302 whilst on a voyage from Halifax N.S.to Liverpool with a cargo
of timber.

BRIARWOOD as ORMINSTER　　　　　　　　　　　　　　　　　*G. Scott Collection*

52. BRIARWOOD (2) (1923 — 1928)

ON. 118651. 3638g, 2362n, 343.3 x 50.1 x 23.5 feet.
T.3-cyl. by Blair and Co. Ltd., Stockton on Tees.
3.1905: Completed by R. Stephenson and Co. Ltd., Newcastle upon Tyne as RELIANCE for
McIntyre Bros. and Co., Newcastle upon Tyne. *1913:* Sold to Manoravon S.S. Co. Ltd. (Griffiths,
Lewis and Co. managers), Cardiff. *1917:* Sold to Griffiths Lewis S.N. Co. Ltd. (J. C. Gould and
Co. (Steamship Managers) Ltd., managers), Cardiff and renamed GRELBEN. *1919:* Sold to
Marine Transport Co. Ltd. (T. B. Humphries manager), Cardiff. *1920:* Management transferred to
W. H. Kelynack and renamed DEEMSTER. *1921:* Management transferred to F. Edwards and Co.
1923: Purchased by Joseph Constantine S.S. Line Ltd. and renamed BRIARWOOD. *1928:* Sold
to P. Regier (K. Behrsing manager), Latvia and renamed SELONIA. *1928:* Sold to Parobrodarsko
Akcionarsko Drustvo 'Progres,' Yugoslavia and renamed OREBIC, *1935:* Sold to Minster S.S. Co
Ltd., London and renamed ORMINSTER, *1936:* Sold to Soc. Anon, di Nav. 'Mare Nostrum', Italy
and renamed COMITAS. *22.9.1939:* Mined off Flushing and beached. *1.1940:* Abandoned as a
total loss.

53. LEVENWOOD (2) (1924 — 1944)
ON. 147768. 803g, 374n, 186.5 × 29.4 × 12.4 feet.
T.3-cyl. by W. Beardmore and Co. Ltd., Coatbridge.
2,1924: Completed by R. Williamson and Son Ltd., Workington for Joseph Constantine S.S. Line
Ltd. *1944:* Sold to Brook Shipping Co. Ltd. (Comben, Longstaff and Co. Ltd. managers), London.
1945: Sold to Williamstown Shipping Co. Ltd. (same managers), London and renamed
DEVONBROOK. *28.8.1946:* Wrecked off Blyth whilst on a voyage from London to Blyth in
ballast.

LEVENWOOD

World Ship Photo Library

54. LARCHWOOD (2) (1924 — 1932)
ON. 147771. 914g, 504n, 198.0 × 32.3 × 12.5 feet.
T.3-cyl. by G. Clark Ltd., Sunderland.
7.1924: Completed by Osbourne, Graham and Co. Ltd., Sunderland for Joseph Constantine S.S.
Line Ltd. *27.1.1932:* Sank following a collision 14 miles S. of Flamborough Head whilst on a
voyage from Leith to London with a cargo of coal.

KINGSWOOD as HOGLAND

A. Duncan

55. KINGSWOOD (2) (1924 — 1928)
ON. 132897. 4250g, 2707n, 363.1 × 51.0 × 26.3 feet.
T.3-cyl. by the Shipbuilders.
1.1914: Completed by J. Readhead and Sons Ltd., South Shields as ONWEN for W. and C. T.
Jones S.S. Co. Ltd. (W. and C. T. Jones managers), Cardiff. *1918: :* Sold to Woolston S.S. Co.
Ltd. (S. Instone and Co. Ltd., managers), Cardiff. *1920:* Sold to Rumney S.S. Co. Ltd. (same
managers), Cardiff and renamed RUMNEY. *1924:* Purchased by Joseph Constantine S.S. Line
Ltd. and renamed KINGSWOOD. *1928:* Sold to A/B, Naxos Prince (R. Mattson, manager), Finland
and renamed HOGLAND. *1935:* Management transferred to Curt Mattson. *21.8.1941:*
Torpedoed and sunk by the French submarine RUBIS whilst on a voyage from Norway to a
German Baltic port with a cargo of iron ore.

QUEENSWOOD as **ARRAIZ**   *H. S. Appleyard Collection*

56. QUEENSWOOD (2) (1925 — 1932)
ON. 147776. 4537g, 2790n, 370.0 × 56.3 × 25.4 feet.
T.3-cyl. by Central Marine Engine Works, West Hartlepool.
3.1925: Completed by New Waterway Shipbuilding Co., Schiedam for Joseph Constantine S.S.
Line Ltd. *1932:* Sold to Cia. Nav. Vascongada, Spain and renamed ARRAIZ. *1972:* Sold to
Aguilar y Peris and broken up by Industrial y Comercial de Levante S.A. who commenced
demolition during *6.1972* at Valencia.

COPSEWOOD as **KYLEBANK**   *World Ship Photo Library*

57. COPSEWOOD (3) (1925 — 1939)
ON. 147777, 969g, 537n, 198.0 × 32.3 × 12.4 feet.
T.3-cyl. by G. Clark Ltd., Sunderland.
4.1925: Completed by Osbourne, Graham and Co. Ltd., Sunderland for Joseph Constantine S.S.
Line Ltd. *1939:* Sold to Kyle Shipping Co. Ltd. (Monroe Bros., managers), Liverpool and renamed
KYLEBANK. *1958:* Sold to N. V. Scheepswerf Gruno who commenced demolition during *4.1958*
at Foxhol.

HOMEWOOD as HOLDERNOOK   *World Ship Photo Library*

58. HOMEWOOD (3) (1927 — 1939)
ON. 147785. 870g, 426n, 188.3 × 30.2 × 12.4 feet.
T.3-cyl. by W. Beardmore and Co. Ltd., Coatbridge.
1.1927: Completed by R. Williamson and Son Ltd., Workington for Joseph Constantine S.S. Line
Ltd. *1939:* Sold to Kyle Shipping Co. Ltd. (Monroe Bros., managers), Liverpool and renamed
KYLEBROOK. *1942:* Sold to Northwest Shipping Co. Ltd. (Joseph Constantine S.S. Line Ltd.,
managers), Workington. *1945:* Sold to Ellerman's Wilson Line Ltd., Hull. *1946:* Renamed
DYNAMO. *1956:* Sold to Holderness S.S. Co. Ltd., Hull and renamed HOLDERNOOK. *18.8.1959:*
Arrived at Haarlem to be broken up by M. C. Hoole.

HAZELWOOD   *H. S. Appleyard Collection*

59. HAZELWOOD (2) (1927 — 1937)
ON. 147792. 3744g, 2270n, 366.1 × 52.5 × 22.1 feet.
T.3-cyl. by the Shipbuilders.
8.1927: Completed by J. Readhead and Sons Ltd., South Shields for Joseph Constantine S.S.
Line Ltd. *1934:* Lengthened to 388.8 feet with the fitting of a Maierform bow and tonnages
increased to 3889g. and 2335n. *1937:* Sold to Brodarsko Akcionarsko Drustvo 'Oceania',
Yugoslavia and renamed SUSAK. *6.6.1942:* Torpedoed and sunk by the Japanese submarine
I.16 in a position 15.42S. 40.58E. whilst on a voyage from Aden to Lourenco Marques.

KIRNWOOD   *A. Duncan*

KIRNWOOD with Maierform bow   *Company Archives*

60. KIRNWOOD (2) (1928 — 1941)
ON. 147794. 3741g, 2272n, 366.5 × 52.5 × 22.0 feet.
T.3-cyl. by the Shipbuilders.
1.1928: Completed by J. Readhead and Sons Ltd., South Shields for Joseph Constantine S.S. Line Ltd. *1935:* Lengthened to 389.6 feet with the fitting of a Maierform bow and tonnages increased to 3829g. and 2359n. *10.12.1941:* Torpedoed and sunk by the German submarine U.130 in a position 56.57N. 16.35W. whilst on a voyage from New York and Sydney N.S. to Ipswich.

TOFTWOOD   *A. Duncan*

61. TOFTWOOD (3) (1928 — 1936)
ON. 147795. 4302g, 2669n, 378.0 × 52.5 × 25.3 feet.
T. 3-cyl. by Swan, Hunter and Wigham Richardson Ltd., Newcastle upon Tyne.
1.1928: Completed by Swan, Hunter and Wigham Richardson Ltd., Sunderland for Joseph
Constantine S.S. Line Ltd. *1936:* Sold to Alexandria Nav. Co. S.A.E., Egypt and renamed STAR
OF ALEXANDRIA. *1950:* Sold to Bruno and Eredi Arturo Montanari, Italy and renamed
MONTARDIZIO. *1959:* Sold to Cie Miniere et Metallurgique, Morocco and renamed KETTARA II.
1959: Sold to Naigai Unyu K. K. who commenced demolition *30.11.1959* at Kure.

GOODWOOD

World Ship Photo Library

62. GOODWOOD (2) (1928 — 1936)
ON. 147796. 5008g, 3089n, 401.2 × 55.0 × 25.6 feet.
T. 3-cyl. by the Shipbuilders.
2.1928: Completed by J. Readhead and Sons Ltd., South Shields for Joseph Constantine S. S.
Line Ltd. *1936:* Sold to Drake Shipping Co. Ltd., London and renamed MERCHANT ROYAL.
3.7.1946: Sank in tow 10 miles off Portland Bill following a collision with the American steamer
WILLIAM B. TRAVIS, 7176/42 in a position 50.21N. 02.29W. whilst on a voyage from St. John
N.B. to Hull with a cargo of steel and timber.

KINGSWOOD

Company Archives

63. KINGSWOOD (3) (1929 — 1943)
ON. 160723. 5055g, 3077n, 405.4 × 53.8 × 26.6 feet.
T. 3-cyl. by North Eastern Marine Engineering Co. Ltd., Newcastle upon Tyne.
5.1929: Completed by Northumberland Shipbuilding Co. (1927) Ltd., Newcastle upon Tyne for
Joseph Constantine S.S. Line Ltd. *17.12.1943:* Torpedoed and sunk by the German submarine
U.515 in a position 05.57 N. 01.43E. in the Gulf of Guinea.

BROOKWOOD at Mombasa in 1935   *Brownell Collection*

64. BROOKWOOD (2) (1929 — 1940)
ON. 160724. 5082g, 3088n, 408.2 × 53.5 × 26.3 feet.
T. 3-cyl. by Central Marine Engine Works, West Hartlepool.
5.1929: Completed by Wm. Gray and Co. Ltd., West Hartlepool for Joseph Constantine S.S. Line Ltd. *23.8.1940:* Torpedoed and sunk by the German submarine U.37 in a position 54.40N 27.57W.

65. WEARWOOD (2) (1930 — 1946)
ON. 160727. 4578g, 2795n, 382.6 × 52.0 × 26.6 feet.
T. 3-cyl. by North Eastern Marine Engineering Co. Ltd., Newcastle upon Tyne.
1.1930: Completed by Northumberland Shipbuilding Co. (1927) Ltd., Newcastle upon Tyne for Joseph Constantine S. S. Line Ltd. *1946:* Sold to Basra Steam Shipping Co. Ltd. (Galbraith, Pembroke and Co. Ltd. managers), London and renamed HARROW. *1950:* Sold to Stallbergs Grufve Aktiebolags Rederi (Per Skiold manager), Sweden and renamed IDKERBERG. *1957:* Sold to Rederiet For S.S. Carita (J. E. Manne and Co. managers), Sweden and renamed CARITA. *1962:* Sold to A. Sigalas and Platis Bros., Lebanon and renamed MARGARITI. *18.10.1967:* Grounded off Terschelling after her rudder had broken whilst on a voyage from Szczecin to Alexandria and abandoned as a total loss.

WEARWOOD   *World Ship Photo Library*

MAPLEWOOD
World Ship Photo Library

66. MAPLEWOOD (3) (1930 — 1943)
ON. 160728. 4562g, 2788n, 382.5 × 52.0 × 26.6 feet.
T. 3-cyl. by North Eastern Marine Engineering Co. Ltd., Newcastle upon Tyne.
5.1930: Completed by Northumberland Shipbuilding Co. (1927) Ltd., Newcastle upon Tyne for Joseph Constantine S.S. Line Ltd. *1943:* Sold to Maritime Shipping and Trading Co. Ltd., London. *1945:* Renamed MAPLEDORE. *1960:* Sold to British Iron and Steel Corporation, allocated to John Cashmore Ltd. and arrived at Newport, Mon. *28.6.1960* to be broken up.

67. BRIARWOOD (3) (1930 — 1945)
ON. 160733. 4013g, 2420n, 364.8 × 51.0 × 24.9 feet.
T. 3-cyl. by North Eastern Marine Engineering Co. Ltd., Newcastle upon Tyne.
7.1930: Completed by Northumberland Shipbuilding Co. (1927) Ltd., Newcastle upon Tyne for Constantine Shipping Co. Ltd. *1932:* Transferred to Joseph Constantine S. S. Line Ltd. *1945:* Sold to Stag Line Ltd. (J. Robinson and Sons managers), North Shields. *1946:* Renamed GARDENIA *1964:* Sold to Amfitriti Cia. Nav. S.A., Panama and renamed AIS NICOLAS. *1965:* Sold to Astrosplendor Cia. Nav. S.A., Panama, *20.10.1968:* Extensively damaged when fire broke out in the engine room whilst undergoing repairs at Port Said and declared a total loss. Sold to Adly Makari and broken up at Port Said.

BRIARWOOD
Company Archives

LINWOOD beached off Cromer after a collision   *P. A. Vicary*

68. LINWOOD (2) (1932 — 1942)
ON. 160735. 992g, 570n, 199.9 × 33.7 × 12.4 feet.
T. 3-cyl. by North Eastern Marine Engineering Co. Ltd., Sunderland.
4.1932: Completed by Burntisland Shipbuilding Co. Ltd., Burntisland for Joseph Constantine
S.S. Line Ltd. *15.11.1942:* Mined and sunk ¼ mile E. of Longsand Buoy in the Thames estuary.

CEDARWOOD in July 1949   *G. A. Osbon*

69. CEDARWOOD (2) (1933 — 1959)
ON. 160737. 899g, 498n, 193.1 × 32.2 × 12.5 feet.
T. 3-cyl. by North Eastern Marine Engineering Co. Ltd., Sunderland.
1933: Completed by Burntisland Shipbuilding Co. Ltd., Burntisland for Joseph Constantine S. S.
Line Ltd. *1947:* Transferred to Constantine Shipping Co. Ltd. *1959:* Sold to N. V. Simons,
Hoogezand and arrived at Delfzyl on *29.9.1959* to be broken up.

PARKWOOD   *Brownell   Collection*

70. PARKWOOD (2) (1933 — 1959)
ON. 160738. 1049g, 585n, 199.9 × 33.2 × 13.6 feet.
T. 3-cyl. by North Eastern Marine Engineering Co. Ltd., Sunderland.
7.1933: Completed by Burntisland Shipbuilding Co. Ltd., Burntisland for Joseph Constantine
S.S. Line Ltd. *1947:* Transferred to Constantine Shipping Co. Ltd. *26.9.1959:* Arrived at Delfzyl
to be broken up by N. V. Scheepswerf Bodewes Gruno.

AVONWOOD   *World Ship Photo Library*

71. AVONWOOD (2) (1934 — 1942)
ON. 160742. 1056g, 597n, 199.8 x 33.2 x 13.6 feet
T.3-cyl. by North Eastern Marine Engineering Co. Ltd., Sunderland.
9.1934: Completed by Burntisland Shipbuilding Co. Ltd., Burntisland for Joseph Constantine
S.S. Line Ltd. *12.12.1942:* Torpedoed and sunk by an E-boat 3 miles from No. 4 Buoy,
Lowestoft.

WESTWOOD   *T. Rayner*

72. WESTWOOD (2) (1935 — 1961)
ON. 164826. 1040g, 595n, 199.9 x 33.3 x 13.6 feet
T.3-cyl. by North Eastern Marine Engineering Co. Ltd., Sunderland.
8.1935: Completed by Burntisland Shipbuilding Co. Ltd., Burntisland for Joseph Constantine
S.S. Line Ltd., *1947:* Transferred to Constantine Shipping Co. Ltd. *31.3.1961:* Arrived at New
Waterway, Holland in tow of the tug ERIMUS CROSS and broken up by N. V. de Koophandel at
Nieuw Lekkerland.

73. WINDSORWOOD (1936 — 1940)
ON. 164828. 5395g, 3147n, 438.9 x 55.8 x 24.8 feet.
T.3-cyl. by North Eastern Marine Engineering Co. Ltd., Newcastle upon Tyne.
6.1936: Completed by Hawthorn, Leslie and Co. Ltd., Newcastle upon Tyne for Constantine
Shipping Co. Ltd. *25.6.1940:* Torpedoed and sunk by the German submarine U.51 in a position
48.31N. 14.50W. whilst on a voyage from R. Tyne to Sierra Leone.

WINDSORWOOD   *World Ship Photo Library*

YORKWOOD   *H. S. Appleyard Collection*

74. YORKWOOD (1) (1936 — 1943)
ON. 164829. 5401g, 3150n, 438.9 x 55.8 x 24.8 feet
T.3-cyl. by North Eastern Marine Engineering Co. Ltd., Newcastle upon Tyne.
7.1936: Completed by Hawthorn, Leslie and Co. Ltd., Newcastle upon Tyne for Constantine
Shipping Co. Ltd., *1942:* Transferred to Joseph Constantine S.S. Line Ltd. *8.1.1943:* Torpedoed
and sunk by the German submarine U.507 in a position 04.10S. 35.30W. whilst on a voyage
from Durban and Table Bay to U.K. via Paranam.

75. NORTHWOOD (1936 — 1959)
ON. 164832. 1146g, 652n, 217.4 x 34.0 x 13.6 feet
T.3-cyl. by North Eastern Marine Engineering Co. Ltd., Sunderland.
10.1936: Completed by Burntisland Shipbuilding Co. Ltd., Burntisland for Joseph Constantine
S.S. Line Ltd. *1947:* Transferred to Constantine Shipping Co. Ltd. *1959:* Sold to N.V.
Machinehandel en Scheeps, de Koophandel who commenced demolition during *10.1959* at
Nieuw Lekkerland.

NORTHWOOD in July 1956   *G. A. Osbon*

SOUTHWOOD   *World Ship Photo Library*

76. SOUTHWOOD (1937 — 1962)
ON, 164834. 1149g, 652n, 217.4 x 34.0 x 13.6 feet
T.3-cyl. by North Eastern Marine Engineering Co. Ltd., Sunderland.
1.1937: Completed by Burntisland Shipbuilding Co. Ltd., Burntisland for Joseph Constantine
S.S. Line Ltd. *1947:* Transferred to Constantine Shipping Co. Ltd. *1962:* Sold to Takis Cia. Nav.
S.A., Panama and renamed EASTPORT. *1965:* Sold to Francisco Fafuente Lozano who
commenced demolition *18.2.1965* at Puerto de Santa Maria, near Bilbao.

77. BALMORALWOOD (1937 — 1940)
ON. 164835. 5834g, 3374n, 446.7 x 56.7 x 26.1 feet
T.3-cyl. by North Eastern Marine Engineering Co. Ltd., Newcastle upon Tyne.
2.1937 Completed by Hawthorn, Leslie and Co. Ltd., Newcastle upon Tyne for Constantine
Shipping Co. Ltd. *14.6.1940:* Torpedoed and sunk by the German submarine U.47 in a position
50.19N. 10.28W. whilst on a voyage from Sorel to Falmouth.

BALMORALWOOD   *World Ship Photo Library*

78. EDENWOOD (3) (1938 — 1939)

ON. 164839. 1167g, 645n, 217.8 x 34.0 x 13.0 feet
4-cyl. 2 S.C.S.A. oil engine by British Auxiliaries Ltd., Glasgow.
2.1938: Completed by G. Brown and Co. (Marine) Ltd., Greenock for Joseph Constantine S.S. Line Ltd. *24.12.1939:* Sank off Nab Tower following a collision with the British motorship DERBYSHIRE, 11660/35 whilst on a voyage from Seaham to Portsmouth with a cargo of coal.

EDENWOOD as built
Brownell Collection

79. EDENWOOD (4) (1943 — 1960)

ON. 164864. 1874g, 982n, 256.3 x 39.1 x 16.4 feet
6-cyl. 2 S.C.S.A. oil engine by British Auxiliaries Ltd., Glasgow.
10.1943: Completed by Hall, Russell and Co. Ltd., Aberdeen for Joseph Constantine S.S. Line Ltd. *1947:* Transferred to Whimster and Co. Ltd. *1949:* Transferred to Constantine Lines Ltd. *1960:* Sold to Piraeus Shipping Co. Ltd., Greece and renamed PARALOS. *1961:* Sold to G. and N. Angelakis, D. and S. Grigoriou and I. Maltezou, Greece. *1965:* Sold to Constantinos G. Ventouris, Greece and renamed ERGINA VENTOURI. *1972:* Sold to Kimolos Nav. Co. Ltd., Cyprus and renamed APOSTOLOS B. *1974:* Sold to Ventouris Shipping Co. Ltd., Cyprus. *1975:* Sold to Mastrogiorgis Shipping Co. Ltd., Cyprus and renamed MERSINI. *1980:* Sold to D. Kyriazis Bros. who commenced demolition *28.8.1980* at Perama.

AVONWOOD after alteration
A. Duncan

80. AVONWOOD (3) (1944 — 1960)

ON. 169136. 1754g, 932n, 256.3 x 39.1 x 16.4 feet
6-cyl. 2 S.C.S.A. oil engine by British Auxiliaries Ltd., Glasgow.
5.1944: Completed by Hall, Russell and Co. Ltd., Aberdeen for Joseph Constantine S.S. Line Ltd. *1947:* Transferred to Whimster and Co. Ltd. *1949:* Transferred to Constantine Lines Ltd. *1960:* Sold to John Stewart and Co. Shipping Ltd., Glasgow and renamed YEWPARK. *1966:* Sold to Friendship Corp. S.A., Greece and renamed FILIA. *1973:* Transferred to Cypriot registry and renamed ELENI M. *23.8.1973:* Wrecked on the Libyan coast in a position 32.00N. 24.40E. whilst on a voyage from Algiers and Annaba to Alexandria with a cargo of scrap iron.

LEVENWOOD *A. Duncan*

81. LEVENWOOD (3) (1946 — 1961)
ON. 169524. 1058g, 584n, 204.8 × 32.8 × 13.7 feet.
T.3-cyl. by Rankin and Blackmore Ltd., Greenock.
6.1945: Completed by G. Brown and Co. (Marine) Ltd., Greenock as EMPIRE BROMLEY for Ministry of War Transport (John Kelly Ltd., managers). *1946:* Purchased by Joseph Constantine S.S. Line Ltd. and renamed LEVENWOOD. *1947:* Transferred to Constantine Shipping Co. Ltd. *1961:* Sold to Panex (Overseas) Ltd., London and renamed BASILDON. *1962:* Sold to Don Shipping Co. Ltd. (Charles M. Willie and Co. (Shipping) Ltd., managers), London. *1963:* Management transferred to R. S. Briggs and Co. (Shipping) Ltd. *1967:* Sold to Jos. de Smedt who completed demolition *19.10.1967* at Burcht.

82. GARTWOOD (1946 — 1966)
ON. 169484. 2414g, 1282n, 282.2 × 40.5 × 18.7 feet.
8-cyl. 2 S.C.S.A. oil engine by British Polar Engines Ltd., Glasgow.
10.1946: Completed by Burntisland Shipbuilding Co. Ltd., Burntisland for Whimster and Co. Ltd. *1949:* Transferred to Constantine Lines Ltd. *1964:* Transferred to Constantine Shipping Co. Ltd. *1966:* Sold to N. Vlachos and N. Makrynos, Greece and renamed AGIOS NICOLAOS. *1981:* Sold to D. Kyriazis Bros., who commenced demolition *16.6.1981* at Perama.

GARTWOOD *A. Duncan*

LOCHWOOD

Brownell Collection

83. LOCHWOOD (2) (1949 — 1963)
ON. 182138. 1689g, 852n, 275.4 × 41.7 × 15.3 feet.
8-cyl. 2 S.C.S.A. oil engine by British Polar Engines Ltd., Glasgow.
11.1949: Completed by Burntisland Shipbuilding Co. Ltd., Burntisland for Wood Lines Ltd.
1962: Transferred to Constantine Lines (Operations) Ltd. *1963:* Sold to Atlantska Plovidba,
Yugoslavia and renamed LAPAD. *1970:* Sold to Mediteranska Plovidba, Yugoslavia. *1971:* Sold
to Brodospas who commenced demolition *27.4.1971* at Split.

84. ESKWOOD (2) (1951 — 1967)
ON. 169158. 1273g, 667n, 226′ 2″ × 35′ 6″ × 15′ 8½″.
4-cyl. 2 S.C.S.A. oil engine by British Polar Engines Ltd., Glasgow.
11.1951: Completed by Burntisland Shipbuilding Co. Ltd., Burntisland for Constantine Shipping
Co. Ltd. *1967:* Sold to Avlis Shipping Co. Special S.A., Greece and renamed ASTYANAX. *1969:*
Sold to Prodromos Shipping Co. S.A., Greece and renamed KASSANDRA. *1976:* Sold to Panacar
Navigation Co. Ltd., Cyprus and renamed EVANGELOS. *1979:* Sold to Thadem Shipping Co. Ltd.,
Cyprus. *31.1.1980:* Abandoned and sank in a position 36.25N. 21.15E. after developing leaks
whilst on a voyage from Beirut to Hamburg.

ESKWOOD

Brownell Collection

COPSEWOOD   *World Ship Photo Library*

85. COPSEWOOD (4) (1951 — 1967)
ON 169159. 1272g, 667n, 226' 1" × 35' 6" × 15' 8¾"
4-cyl. 2 S.C.S.A. oil engine by British Polar Engines Ltd., Glasgow.
11.1951: Completed by Burntisland Shipbuilding Co. Ltd., Burntisland for Constantine Shipping Co. Ltd. *1967:* Sold to Knossos Shipping Co. Ltd., Cyprus and renamed DORA. *1970:* Sold to Alkmini Shipping Co. Ltd., Cyprus and renamed RIGEL. *3.11.1970:* Beached on a sandbank 2 miles off Texel after developing engine trouble during a storm whilst on a voyage from Terneuzen to Lubeck. She subsequently capsized and sank after sliding off the sandbank.

86. TEESWOOD (4) (1953 — 1956)
ON. 169160. 1246g, 633n, 226' 2" × 35' 6" × 15' 8½"
5-cyl. 2 S.C.S.A. oil engine by British Polar Engines Ltd., Glasgow.
9.1953: Completed by Burntisland Shipbuilding Co. Ltd., Burntisland for Constantine Shipping Co. Ltd. *29.7.1956:* Abandoned by her crew and capsized in heavy weather 4 miles E. of Dungeness whilst on a voyage from Blyth to Shoreham with a cargo of coal. *31.7.1956:* Sank 2 miles off Dover.

TEESWOOD   *Brownell Collection*

TYNEWOOD

87. TYNEWOOD (1957 — 1967)
ON. 187308. 1495g, 657n, 237' 1" × 38' 1" × 15' 6"
8-cyl. 2 S.C.S.A. oil engine by H. Widdop and Co. Ltd., Keighley.
2.1957: Completed by Ailsa Shipbuilding Co. Ltd., Troon for Constantine Shipping Co. Ltd.
1967: Sold to Chimica Mare Soc. di Nav., Italy and renamed SU NURAXI. Converted to a tanker.
1968: Sold to Chemicals S.p.A. di Navigazione, Italy. *1972:* Sold to Petrolchimica di Navigazione
S.p.A., Italy. *1979:* Sold to Diana S.r.l., Italy and renamed FRAI. Still in service.

88. THAMESWOOD (1957 — 1968)
ON. 187311. 1799g, 894n, 270' 9" × 38' 7" × 17' 0"
8-cyl. 2 S.C.S.A. oil engine by H. Widdop and Co. Ltd., Keighley.
11.1957: Completed by Ailsa Shipbuilding Co. Ltd., Troon for Constantine Shipping Co. Ltd.
1968: Sold to Chemicals S.p.A. di Navigazione, Italy and renamed SERRA ORRIOS. Converted
to a tanker. *1972:* Sold to Petrolchimica di Navigazione S.p.A., Italy and renamed CHEMICAL
ORRIOS, *1977:* Renamed SERRA ORRIOS. *1979:* Sold to Iago S.r.l., Italy and renamed IAGO.
Still in service.

THAMESWOOD

HIGHLINER   *Brownell Collection*

89. HIGHLINER (1959 — 1966)
ON. 187315. 3349g, 1786n, 326' 1" × 46' 8" × 20' 10"
Two C.2-cyl. by the Shipbuilder driving a single shaft.
1948: Completed by Smiths' Dock Co. Ltd., Middlesbrough as MABELLA for A/S. Mabella (Karl Bruusgaard manager), Norway. *1959:* Purchased by Teesdale S.S. Co. Ltd. and renamed HIGHLINER. *1964:* Transferred to Tynedale Shipping Co. Ltd. *1966:* Sold to Cocconis Nav. Co. Ltd., Cyprus and renamed VIRGIN MARY. *1967:* Sold to Pasparo Shipping Co. Ltd., Cyprus and renamed PETROS. *12.6.1972:* Arrived at Newport, Mon. in tow from Cardiff to be broken up by John Cashmore Ltd. She had been laid up at Cardiff since *20.1.1971.*

YORKWOOD as **BENIN**   *A. Duncan*

90. YORKWOOD (2) (1960 — 1964)
ON. 183786. 2483g, 1282n, 312' 0" × 44' 2" × 17' 8"
T.3-cyl. by Rankin and Blackmore Ltd., Greenock.
8.1950: Completed by J. Lamont and Co. Ltd., Port Glasgow as BENIN for Elder, Dempster Lines Ltd., Liverpool. *1960:* Purchased by Tynedale Shipping Co. Ltd. and renamed YORKWOOD. *1964:* Sold to Mediterranean and Baltic Shipping Corp., Greece and renamed NOUFARO. *1968:* Sold to Agia Irene Steamship Corp., Greece and renamed AGIA IRENE. *23.7.1969:* Foundered in Corunna Roads after developing leaks in heavy weather whilst on a voyage from Huelva to Ghent.

EASTWOOD

91. EASTWOOD (1960 — 1968)
ON. 301425. 1793g, 905n, 271′0″ × 38′8″ × 17′0″
8-cyl. 2 S.C.S.A. oil engine by H. Widdop and Co. Ltd., Keighley.
10.1960: Completed by Ailsa Shipbuilding Co. Ltd., Troon for Constantine Shipping Co. Ltd.
1968: Sold to Chemicals S.p.A. di Navigazione, Italy and renamed PALMAVERA. Converted to
a tanker. *1972:* Sold to Petrolchimica di Navigazione S.p.A., Italy. *1979:* Renamed DAMA. *1981:*
Sold to Z.A.R. S.r.l., Italy. Still in service.

ABBOT as **IVYTOWN**   *A. Duncan*

M.1. ABBOT (1917 — 1918)
ON. 115631. 264g, 104n, 142.5 × 21.3 × 10.2 feet.
C. 2-cyl. by A. Rodger and Co., Glasgow.
4.1903: Completed by J. Fullerton and Co., Paisley for Frontier Town S.S. Co. Ltd. (J. Fisher and Sons managers), Newry. *1915:* Sold to Llewellyn and Evans, Cardiff. *1915:* Sold to Care and Young Shipping Co. Ltd., Cardiff. *1916:* Sold to W. A. Jenkins and Co., Swansea. *1916:* Sold to E. Wilford, London. *1917:* Sold to Channel Transport Ltd. (Stone and Rolfe Ltd. managers), Llanelly. *1917:* Sold to Abbot Shipping Co. Ltd. (R. A. Constantine and T. H. Donking managers). *1918:* Management transferred to Stone and Rolfe Ltd., Llanelly. *1919:* Sold to Town Line (London) Ltd. (Harrison, Sons and Co. managers), Cardiff and renamed IVYTOWN. *1924:* Sold to N. B. Leslie, Dundee. *1924:* Sold to Great Yarmouth Shipping Co. Ltd., Great Yarmouth. *1927:* Sold to A. Ogg, Aberdeen. *1928:* Sold to Steam Coasters Ltd., Cardiff. *1935:* Sold to A. Simpson (Comben, Longstaff and Co. Ltd. managers), London. *1935:* Sold to unnamed Greek owners and renamed BALTIK. *1935:* Sold to Brook Shipping Co. Ltd. (Comben, Longstaff and Co. Ltd. managers), London and renamed KENTBROOK. *26.12.1935:* Sailed from Plymouth on a voyage to Portsmouth with a cargo of stone and subsequently disappeared.

M.2. RENEN (1917 — 1918)
ON. 142387. 656g, 354n, 179.6 × 27.7 × 14.1 feet.
2 cylinder steam engine by T. Richardson and Sons, Hartlepool. Replaced in 1879 by a C. 2-cyl. by Flensburger Schiffsbau Ges., Flensburg.
1869: Completed by Denton, Gray and Co., West Hartlepool as PRIMA for Flensburg Steam Navigation Co., Germany. *1883:* Sold to R. Andvord, Norway and renamed PROSPERO. *1886:* Transferred to Ostlandske Lloyd (R. Andvord manager), Norway. *1906:* Sold to Akties. Ganger Rolf (Fred Olsen manager), Norway. *1900:* Sold to O. Wathnes Arvinger, Norway. *1912:* Sold to Akties. Prospero (E. Rusten manager), Norway. *1916:* Sold to Ths. J. Wiborg and Son, Norway and renamed RENEN. *1917:* Taken over by The Shipping Controller (R. A. Constantine and T. H. Donking managers). *1918:* Returned to owners. *26.1.1920:* Sank off Tynemouth following a collision whilst on a voyage from R. Tyne to Tonsberg with a cargo of coke.

M.3. GAULA (1917)
ON. 136034. 1085g, 646n, 223.9 × 33.2 × 15.2 feet.
T. 3-cyl. by the Shipbuilders.
1910: Completed by Bergens Mek. Verksted, Bergen for Kulkompagniet af 1871, Norway. *1917:* Taken over by The Shipping Controller (J. Constantine manager). *1917:* Returned to owners. *1922:* Sold to D/S. A/S. Gaula (Kulkompagniet af 1871 managers), Norway. *1928:* Sold to Egil Naesheim, Norway and renamed VARILD. *22.1.1940:* Sailed from Horten on a voyage to Sunderland in ballast and subsequently disappeared.

M.4. NORFOLK (1917 — 1919)
ON. 136082. 3775g, 2349n, 344.0 × 49.1 × 24.9 feet.
T. 3-cyl. by North Eastern Marine Engineering Co. Ltd., Sunderland.
1907: Completed by J. Priestman and Co., Sunderland for Harloff and Rodseth, Norway. *1915:* Sold to A/S. Klosters Rederi (L. Kloster manager), Norway. *1917:* Taken over by The Shipping Controller (Constantine and Pickering S.S. Co. Ltd. managers). *1919:* Returned to owners, *1920:* Sold to A/S. Det Selmerske Rederi, Norway and renamed ROWENA. *1928:* Sold to A/S. Norasiatic Coal Transports Ltd. (C. L. Halvorsen manager), Norway. *1930:* Management transferred to E. M. Nilsen Moe, *1934:* Sold to N. E. A. Moller, Shanghai and renamed NANCY MOLLER. *1935:* Transferred to Moller Line Ltd. *1936:* Mollers' Ltd. appointed managers. *18.3.1944:* Torpedoed and sunk by the Japanese submarine I.165 in a position 02.14N. 78.25E. whilst on a voyage from Durban to Colombo.

M.5. KUL (1917 — 1918)
ON. 136083. 1095g, 639n, 224.7 × 34.2 × 14.0 feet.
T. 3-cyl. by Ross and Duncan, Glasgow.
1900: Completed by Russell and Co., Port Glasgow as GARONNE for Dampskibsselsk. Garonne (Fearnley and Eger managers), Norway. *1912:* Sold to A/S. Kistransport (Thv. Halvorsen manager), Norway and renamed KUL. *1917:* Taken over by The Shipping Controller (Constantine and Pickering S.S. Co. Ltd. managers). *12.6.1918:* Torpedoed and sunk by a German submarine $3\frac{1}{2}$ miles N.E. of Wolf Rock whilst on a voyage from Swansea to Rouen with a cargo of coal.

M.6. STRYN (1918).
ON. 142304. 2143g, 1346n, 281.3 × 40.3 × 19.8 feet.
T. 3-cyl. by Blair and Co. Ltd., Stockton on Tees.
1901: Completed by Bonn and Mees, Rotterdam as LOUISE for Maats. S. S. Louise (P. W. Louwman manager), Holland. *1915:* Sold to Akties. Fragtfart (J. Kjode Akties, managers), Norway and renamed STRYN. *1918:* Taken over by The Shipping Controller (Constantine, Donking and Co. managers).*10.6.1918:* Torpedoed and sunk 5 miles E. of Berry Head by the German submarine UB.80 whilst on a voyage from Rouen to Barry in ballast.

M.7. MERCATOR (1918 — 1919)
ON. 142361. 999g, 609n, 212.4 × 33.2 × 13.7 feet.
T. 3-cyl. by the Shipbuilders.
5.1910: Completed by Rotterdamsche Droogdok Maats., Rotterdam as MOORDRECHT for Stoomv. Maats. de Maas (Ph. van Ommeren managers), Holland. *1917:* Sold to N. V. Van der Eb and Dresselhuy's Scheepv. Maats., Holland and renamed MERCATOR. *1918:* Taken over by The Shipping Controller (R. A. Constantine and T. H. Donking managers). *1919:* Returned to Stoomv. Maats. de Maas (Ph. van Ommeren managers). *1919:* Sold to L. Castel, France and renamed MADO. *1922:* Sold to Soc. Intercontinentale de Transports, France. *1924:* Sold to Chargeurs du Midi, France. *1924:* Sold to Soc. Maritime Nationale, France. *1934:* Sold to Ubaldo Gennari fu Torquato, Italy and renamed TENACIA GENNARI. *1945:* Handed over to unnamed Yugoslav owners at Trieste and subsequently deleted from the register.

M.8. EDNA (1918 — 1919)
ON. 142592. 1025g, 628n, 210.0 × 34.3 × 14.1 feet.
T. 3-cyl. by the Shipbuilders.
1909: Completed by Flensburger Schiffsbau — Gesellschaft, Flensburg as PRESIDENT CORTY for Cie. Belge Scandinave de Nav. a Vap., Belgium. *1911:* Sold to Dampskibsselsk. af 1911 (H. A. Christensen manager), Denmark and renamed EDNA. *1918:* Taken over by The Shipping Controller (R. A. Constantine and T. H. Donking managers), *1919:* Returned to owners. *1920:* Sold to A/S. Det Forenede Bugserselskab (R. Dobel manager), Denmark and renamed SLIEN. *1922:* Sold to Rob. M. Sloman Jnr., Germany and renamed SESTRI. *1925:* Sold to Flensburg — Stettiner Dampfsch. Ges., Germany and renamed SILVIA. *1929:* Sold to Lubeck-Wyburger Dampfsch. Ges., Germany and renamed ESCHENBURG. *9.3.1954:* Arrived at Hamburg to be broken up by Lehr and Co.

VESSELS MANAGED 1939 - 1951

M.9. RAVONIA (1939 — 1944)
ON. 140833. 813g, 378n, 186.5 × 29.4 × 12.4 feet.
T. 3-cyl. by W. Beardmore and Co. Ltd., Coatbridge.
4.1925: Completed by R. Williamson and Son Ltd., Workington for Northwest Shipping Co. Ltd. (R. Williamson manager), Workington. *1939:* Management transferred to Joseph Constantine S.S. Line Ltd. *23.9.1944:* Sank off the Humber Estuary following a collision with a British destroyer whilst on a voyage from Sunderland to London.

CORINIA *Brownell Collection*

M.10. CORINIA (1939 — 1941)
ON. 140835. 870g, 426n, 188.3 × 30.2 × 12.4 feet.
T. 3-cyl. by W. Beardmore and Co. Ltd., Coatbridge.
10.1928: Completed by R. Williamson and Son Ltd., Workington for Northwest Shipping Co. Ltd.
(R. Williamson manager), Workington. *1939:* Management transferred to Joseph Constantine S.
S. Line Ltd. *10.3.1941:* Mined and sunk in the Straits of Dover in a position 50.55N. 00.35E.

GALACUM *Brownell Collection*

M.11. GALACUM (1939 — 1945)
ON. 133263. 585g, 243n, 165.7 × 26.6 × 11.0 feet.
T. 3-cyl. by Ross and Duncan, Glasgow.
11.1915: Completed by R. Williamson and Son, Workington for their own account, *1923:*
Registered under Northwest Shipping Co. Ltd. (R. Williamson manager), Workington. *1939:*
Management transferred to Joseph Constantine S.S. Line Ltd. *1945:* Sold to Derwent Steam
Shipping Co. Ltd. (Anthony and Bainbridge Ltd. managers), Newcastle upon Tyne. *1951:* Sold to
Satco Shipping Co. Ltd., London and renamed SATCO PREFECT. *1952:* Sold to Tyson, Edgar
Shipping Co. Ltd., London. *5.1954:* Sold to British Iron and Steel Corporation, allocated to C. W.
Dorkin and Co. and broken up at Redheugh on Tyne.

M.12. KYLEBROOK (1942 — 1945)
See HOMEWOOD (No. 58).

M.13. S.N.A. 10 (1940 — 1945)
ON. 166302. 2921g, 1812n, 316.4 × 46.6 × 21.1 feet.
T. 3-cyl. by the Shipbuilders.
1920: Completed by Ateliers et Chantiers de la Loire, Nantes as LOUIS NAIL for French
Government. *1922:* Sold to Cie. Industrielle Maritime, France and renamed LAPEYRADE. *1923:*

Sold to Cie. Navale Industrielle, France. *1937:* Sold to Soc. Nationale d'Affretements, France and renamed S.N.A. 10. *17.7.1940:* Requisitioned at Liverpool by Ministry of Shipping, later Ministry of War Transport (Joseph Constantine S.S. Line Ltd. managers). *1945:* Returned to owners. *1951:* Sold to Soc. Nav. Bordelaise (Cie. Mar. et Com. du Sud-Ouest managers), France and renamed LEOGNAN. *1958:* Sold to French shipbreakers and arrived at Havre *27.2.1958* to be broken up.

M.14. ERNA III (1940 — 1941)
ON. 167609. 1590g, 924n, 253.5 × 39.1 × 17.6 feet.
Two C. 2-cyl. by the Shipbuilders driving a single shaft.
1930: Completed by Helsingors Jernskibs & Maskinbyggeri A/S., Elsinore as ERNA for J. Lauritzen, Denmark. *1940:* Requisitioned by Ministry of Shipping, later Ministry of War Transport (Joseph Constantine S.S. Line Ltd. managers) and renamed ERNA III, *12.9.1941:* Sailed from Milford Haven for Montreal and *21.9.1941* reported in heavy weather and unable to keep up with the convoy. *22.9.1941:* Torpedoed and sunk by the German submarine U.562 in a position 61.45N. 35.15W.

BENWOOD   *World Ship Photo Library*

M.15. BENWOOD (1940 — 1942)
3931g, 2389n, 344.9 × 51.3 × 25.3 feet.
T. 3-cyl. by North Eastern Marine Engineering Co. Ltd., Sunderland.
1.1910: Completed by Craig, Taylor and Co. Ltd., Stockton on Tees for Joseph Hoult and Co. Ltd., Liverpool. *1913:* Transferred to Steam Transport Co. Ltd. (J. Hoult and Co. Ltd. managers), Liverpool. *1915:* Sold to Adam S.S. Co. Ltd., Aberdeen. *1916:* Sold to London—American Maritime Trading Co. Ltd. (Petersen and Co. Ltd. managers), London. *1922:* Sold to Skjelbreds Rederei A/S. (O.A.T. Skjelbred manager), Norway. *1939:* Management transferred to Kr. Knudsen. *1940:* Placed under management of Joseph Constantine S. S. Line Ltd. *9.4.1942:* Beached following a collision off Molasses Reef, Florida whilst on a voyage from Key West to Hampton Roads and declared a constructive total loss.

LYSAKER IV as **CHICAGO**   *Brownell Collection*

M.16. LYSAKER IV (1940 — 1945)
1551g, 973n, 245.6 × 38.6 × 15.4 feet.
T. 3-cyl. by Ross and Duncan Ltd., Glasgow.
9.1924: Completed by Furness Shipbuilding Co. Ltd., Haverton Hill on Tees as VALE OF

MOWBRAY for Vale Shipping Co. Ltd., Middlesbrough. *1935:* Sold to L. Lorentzen, Norway and renamed LYSAKER IV. *1940:* Placed under management of Joseph Constantine S. S. Line Ltd. *1945:* Returned to owners. *1953:* Renamed CHICAGO. *1954:* Sold to Gennaro Ievoli fu Domenico, Italy and renamed GENNARO IEVOLI. *1958:* Sold to Lorenzo de Medici, Italy and renamed VILLANOVA. *1966:* Sold to S.p.A. Cantieri Nav. del Golfo who commenced demolition *26.2.1966* at La Spezia.

M.17. LYSAKER V (1940 — 1945)
1571g, 888n, 246.6 x 37.9 x 18.2 feet.
C. 2-cyl. by the Shipbuilders.
1936: Completed by Porsgrunds Mek. Vaerksted., Porsgrunn for L. Lorentzen, Norway. *1940:* Placed under management of Joseph Constantine S. S. Line Ltd. *1945:* Returned to owners. *1952:* Sold to Skibsaksjeselsk Bratsberg (Finn Rogenaes manager), Norway and renamed KYA. *1956:* Sold to Backers Rederi A/S. (Erling Larsen manager), Norway. *1958:* Sold to A/S. Sandvik (A.C. Olsen manager), Norway and renamed SALTVIK. *1963:* Sold to Kaspar Nilsen Partrederi, Norway and renamed RAMSVIK. *1965:* Sold to Jens Hetland Partrederi, Norway. *1967:* Sold to Bjonndalen Bruk A/S., Norway. *1969:* Sold to Normann Tandberg, Norway. *1974:* Converted for use as a non propelled barge.

M.18. GUNBORG (1940)
1572g, 835n, 269.2 x 40.4 x 16.6 feet.
T. 3-cyl. by the Shipbuilders.
1930: Completed by Oskarshamns Mek. Verkstads, Oskarshamn for Trelleborgs Angf. Nya Aktiebolag (J. Malmros manager), Sweden. *1939:* Sold to Rederi A/B. Sylvia (A. Billner manager), Sweden. *1940:* Placed under management of Joseph Constantine S. S. Line Ltd. *18.10.1940:* Torpedoed and sunk by the German submarine U.99 in a position 57.14N 10.38W. whilst on a voyage from Halifax N. S. to R. Clyde with a cargo of wood pulp.

M.19. ZAAN (1940 — 1945)
1299g, 726n, 237.4 x 36.7 x 15.9 feet.
T. 3-cyl. by Penn and Bauduin, Dordrecht.
4.1921: Completed by N. V. Scheepswerf Baanhoek, Sliedrecht for N. V. Houtvaart (Vinke and Co. managers), Holland *1940:* Placed under management of Joseph Constantine S. S. Line Ltd. *1945:* Returned to owners. *1948:* Managers restyled as Vinke and Zonen. *1955:* Sold to Egon Oldendorff, Germany and renamed GRETKE OLDENDORFF. *1960:* Sold to Alnwick Harmstorff and arrived at Lubeck *14.11.1960* to be broken up.

M.20. SIGYN (1940)
1981g, 1129n, 282.2 x 40.2 x 19.2 feet
T.3-cyl. by Hutson and Son, Glasgow.
11.1897: Completed by Campbeltown Shipbuilding Co., Campbeltown for Wicanders Rederi A/B. (H. Wicander manager), Sweden. *1912:* Sold to Stockholms Rederi, A/B. Svea (Hj. Blomberg manager), Sweden. *1918:* Management transferred to H. Ericson, . *1931:* Sold to Rederi A/B, Sigyn (H. Lundgren, manager), Sweden. *1940:* Placed under management of Joseph Constantine S.S. Line Ltd. *1.8.1940:* Torpedoed and sunk by the German submarine U.59 in a position 56.10N., 09.25W. whilst on a voyage from New Brunswick to Sunderland with a cargo of pit props.

M.21. NYLAND (1940)
1375g, 760n, 250.9 x 41.3 x 14.8 feet.
C. 2-cyl. by the Shipbuilders.
1939: Completed by Nylands Verksted, Oslo for Skibs A/S, Vilhelm Torkildsen's Rederi (Vilhelm Torkildsen manager), Norway. *1940:* Placed under management of Joseph Constantine S.S. Line Ltd. *5.12.1940:* Last sighted off Skerryvore by the Norwegian steamer MARGA, 1583/23 and reported to have been wrecked *6.12.1940* on West Rock, Iona whilst on a voyage from R. Tyne to Canada. Some wreckage bearing the ship's name was discovered two weeks later.

M.22 EMPIRE CRUSADER (1940)
ON. 167405. 1042g, 589n, 224.0 x 33.3 x 13.7 feet.
T.3-cyl. by the Shipbuilders.
1925: Completed by Atlas — Werke A.G., Bremen as LEANDER for Dampfschifffahrts Ges. Neptun, Germany. *9.11.1939:* Captured off Vigo by H.M.S. IRIS. *1940:* Allocated to Ministry of Shipping (Joseph Constantine S.S. Line Ltd., managers) and renamed EMPIRE CRUSADER. *8.8.1940:* Bombed and sunk by German aircraft 15 miles W. of St. Catherine's Point, Isle of Wight.

M.23 EMPIRE BAY (1940 — 1942)
ON. 160786. 2824g, 1576n, 310.6 x 44.4 x 19.4 feet.
T.3-cyl. by Central Marine Engine Works, West Hartlepool.
11.1940: Completed by Wm. Gray and Co. Ltd., West Hartlepool for Ministry of Shipping, later Ministry of War Transport (Joseph Constantine S.S. Line Ltd., managers). *15.1.1942:* Bombed and sunk by German aircraft in the Tees Bay.

EMPIRE SNOW   *National Maritime Museum*

M.24 EMPIRE SNOW (1941 — 1943)
ON. 165999. 6327g, 4592n, 407.0 × 54.7 × 33.2 feet.
T.3-cyl. by D. Rowan and Co. Ltd., Glasgow.
2.1941: Completed by C. Connell and Co. Ltd., Glasgow for Ministry of War Transport (Joseph Constantine S.S. Line Ltd., managers). *1943:* Management transferred to Cairn Line of Steamships Ltd., Newcastle upon Tyne. *1946:* Sold to Cairn Line of Steamships Ltd. (Cairns, Noble and Co., managers), Newcastle upon Tyne and renamed CAIRNAVON. *1961:* Sold to Sirikari Compania Naviera S.A., Lebanon and renamed VERGOLIVADA. *1968:* Sold to Chinese shipbreakers and broken up at Shanghai.

FORT LAC LA RONGE at Bideford in 1945   *Brownell Collection*

M.25. FORT LAC LA RONGE (1942 — 1944)
ON. 169062. 7131g, 4257n, 424.6 × 57.2 × 34.9 feet.
T.3-cyl. by Dominion Engineering Works Ltd., Montreal.
6.1·942: Completed by Burrard D.D. Co. Ltd., Vancouver B.C. for United States War Shipping Administration and bareboat chartered to Ministry of War Transport (Joseph Constantine S.S. Line Ltd., managers). *3.8.1944:* Damaged by a one man torpedo in a position 49.22N. 00.21W. and towed into Appledore. *1948:* Returned to United States Maritime Commission in a damaged condition, sold to British Iron and Steel Corporation and allocated to T. W. Ward Ltd. for breaking up at Briton Ferry where she arrived *16.2.1949.*

M.26. FORT LA REINE (1942)
7133g, 4257n, 424.6 × 57.2 × 34.9 feet.
T.3-cyl. by Dominion Engineering Works Ltd., Montreal.
7.1942: Completed by Burrard D.D. Co. Ltd., Vancouver B.C. for United States War Shipping Administration and bareboat chartered to Ministry of War Transport (Joseph Constantine S.S. Line Ltd., managers). *17.8.1942:* Torpedoed and sunk in a position 18.30N. 75.20W. by the German submarine U.658.

M.27. FORT BUCKINGHAM (1943 — 1944)
ON. 168436. 7122g, 4247n, 424.6 × 57.2 × 34.9 feet.
T.3-cyl. by Dominion Engineering Works Ltd., Montreal.
2.1943: Completed by Burrard D.D. Co. Ltd., Vancouver B.C. for United States War Shipping Administration and bareboat chartered to Ministry of War Transport (Joseph Constantine S.S. Line Ltd., managers). *20.1.1944:* Torpedoed and sunk in the Indian Ocean in a position 08.50N. 66.25E. by the German submarine U.188.

BENJAMIN TAY   *World Ship Photo Library*

M.28 BENJAMIN TAY (1943 — 1951)
ON. 169563. 1814g, 1026n, 250.1 × 42.1 × 18.3 feet.
T.3-cyl. by the Shipbuilders. Replaced in 1953 by an 8-cyl. 2 S.C.S.A. oil engine by Sulzer Bros. Ltd., Winterthur.
1943: Completed by Pacific Bridge Co., Alameda, California for United States War Shipping Administration and bareboat chartered to Ministry of War Transport (Joseph Constantine S.S. Line Ltd., managers). *1951:* Sold to Elder Dempster Lines Ltd., Liverpool and renamed BENUE. *1952:* Sold to D/S. A/S. Anglo (Valdemar Skogland A/S. managers), Norway and renamed ANGLO. *1965:* Sold to D/S. A/S. Ryvingen (Alf Lindo manager), Norway and renamed LINDVANG. *1969:* Sold to Pigi Alexatos, Greece and renamed DANAOS. *1974:* Sold to Greek Eastern Shipping Co. S.A., Greece and renamed VETA. *1975:* Sold to Fanouri Cia. Nav. S.A., Greece and renamed AGHIOS FANOURIOS III. *1980:* Sold to Greek shipbreakers and broken up at Piraeus.

M.29. FORT DAUPHIN (1943 — 1945)
ON. 169565. 7133g, 4245n, 424.6 × 57.2 × 34.9 feet.
T.3-cyl. by John Inglis Co. Ltd., Toronto.
6.1943: Completed by Burrard D.D. Co. Ltd., Vancouver, B.C. for Canadian Government and bareboat chartered to Ministry of War Transport (Joseph Constantine S.S. Line Ltd., managers). *1945:* Management transferred to McCowen and Gross Ltd., London. *1950:* Sold to Watergate S.S. Co. Ltd. (R. S. Dalgliesh Ltd., managers), Newcastle upon Tyne and renamed WARKWORTH. *1957:* Sold to Cia. Mar. Amaconte S.A., Liberia and renamed BODORO. *1959:* Joaquin Ponte Naya S.A., Liberia appointed managers, *27.1.1967:* Beached in Chesapeake Bay following a collision with the American steamer BEAVER STATE, 7650/44 whilst on a voyage from Corcubion to Baltimore. *24.3.1967:* Refloated and *11.5.1967* sold to Peck Iron and Steel Co., Portsmouth, Va. for demolition.

FORT DAUPHIN   *W.S.P.L. Canadian Forces*

CHARLES TREADWELL   *Brownell Collection*

M.30. CHARLES TREADWELL (1943 — 1950)
ON. 169570 1814g, 1019n, 250.0 × 42.1 × 18.3 feet.
T. 3-cyl. by the Shipbuilders.
1943: Completed by Pacific Bridge Co., Alameda, California for United States War Shipping Administration and bareboat chartered to Ministry of War Transport (Joseph Constantine S.S. Line Ltd. managers). *1950:* Sold to Henry P. Lenaghan and Sons Ltd., Belfast and renamed DUNDRUM BAY. *1952:* Sold to Cia. de Navegacion Lore S.A., Panama and renamed ESITO. *1953:* Renamed SANDRA. *1953:* Sold to Sandra Navigation Corp., Liberia and renamed WEST INDIES. *1954:* Sold to Navebras S.A. (Comercio de Petroleo), Brazil and renamed ESITO. *1955:* Sold to Transmaritima Comercial S.A., Brazil. *30.9.1964:* Ran aground at Necochea during a storm, broke in two and became a total loss.

M.31. SAMUEL VERY (1943 — 1951)
ON. 169586. 1814g, 1019n, 250.0 × 42.1 × 18.3 feet.
T. 3-cyl. by the Shipbuilders.
1943: Completed by Pacific Bridge Co., Alameda, California for United States War Shipping Administration and bareboat chartered to Ministry of War Transport (Joseph Constantine S. S. Line Ltd. managers). *1951:* Sold to Adan Shipping Co. Ltd., Montreal and renamed ANGUSLOCH. *1953:* Sold to Republic of Korea and renamed CHANGSUNG. *1954:* Sold to Dai Han Coal Corporation, Korea. *1972:* Sold to Dae Kyung Transportation Co. Ltd., Korea. *1974:* Sold to Korea Industrial Leasing Co. Ltd., Korea. Still in service.

SAMUEL VERY   *G. Scott Collection*

M.32. EMPIRE BERMUDA (1944 — 1946)
ON. 180078. 3539g, 2257n, 315.5 × 46.5 × 22.1 feet.
T. 3-cyl. by Central Marine Engine Works, West Hartlepool.
11.1944: Completed by Wm. Gray and Co. Ltd., West Hartlepool for Ministry of War Transport
(Joseph Constantine S.S. Line Ltd. managers). *1946:* Management transferred to Moller Line
(U.K.) Ltd., London. *1949:* Sold to The Indo-China Steam Navigation Co. Ltd., London and
renamed HEWSANG *1963:* Sold to Sunshine Nav. Co. S.A., Panama and renamed SUNSHINE.
1970: Sold to Taiwan shipbreakers and broken up at Kaohsiung.

EMPIRE BARBADOS as BERYLSTONE   *Real Photographs*

M.33. EMPIRE BARBADOS (1945 — 1946)
ON. 180081. 3538g, 2259n, 315.5 × 46.5 × 22.1 feet.
T. 3-cyl. by Central Marine Engine Works, West Hartlepool.
3.1945: Completed by Wm. Gray and Co. Ltd., West Hartlepool for Ministry of War Transport
(Joseph Constantine S.S. Line Ltd., managers). *1946:* Management transferred to Rodney S.S.
Co. Ltd., London. *1948:* Sold to Rodney S.S. Co. Ltd., London and renamed TENNYSON. *1950:*
Sold to Thomas Stone (Shipping) Ltd., Llanelly and renamed BERYLSTONE. *1955:* Transferred
to Western Carriers Ltd. which was subsequently restyled as Thomas Stone (Shipping) Ltd.
1959: Sold to Zannis Cia. Naviera S.A., Lebanon and renamed MANTICOS. *8.10.1963:* Reported
sinking whilst on a voyage from Libreville to Eastern Mediterranean ports and, after being
abandoned by her crew, drifted ashore in a position 11.14N. 16.52W. and became a total loss.

M.34. EMPIRE CONTEES (1945 — 1946)
1923g, 935n, 280.1 × 44.3 × 26.2 feet.
Two C. 2-cyl. by Rheinmetall-Borsig AG., Berlin Tegel driving a single shaft.
1944: Completed by Akt. Burmeister and Wain, Copenhagen as IRENE OLDENDORFF for Egon
Oldendorff, Germany. *5.1945:* Seized at Lubeck by Allied forces, allocated to Ministry of War
Transport (Joseph Constantine S.S. Line Ltd. managers) and renamed EMPIRE CONTEES. *1946:*
Allocated to U.S.S.R. and renamed OMSK. *1947:* Sold to Zegluga Polska S.A. (Gdynia-American
Shipping Lines Ltd. managers), Poland and renamed OPOLE. *1950:* Sold to Polish Government
for use as a cadet training ship and renamed ZETEMPOWIEC. *1957:* Renamed GRYF.
Subsequently became an unnamed cadet accommodation vessel alongside a Polish Naval base.

FORT LA TOUR as ASSIMINA K.   *Brownell Collection*

M.35. FORT LA TOUR (1949 — 1951)
ON. 169581. 7142g, 4241n, 424.7 x 57.1 x 34.9 feet.
T. 3-cyl. by Dominion Engineering Works Ltd., Montreal.
6.1943: Completed by Marine Industries Ltd., Sorel, P.Q. for Canadian Government and bareboat chartered to Ministry of War Transport (Stephens, Sutton Ltd. managers). *1946:* Management transferred to Wm. Brown, Atkinson and Co. Ltd., Hull. *1949:* Management transferred to Joseph Constantine S.S. Line Ltd. *1951:* Sold to Megantic Freighters Ltd. (J. P. Hadoulis Ltd. managers), London and renamed ASSIMINA K. *1959:* Renamed JEAN BAPTISTE. *1960:* Sold to British Iron and Steel Corporation, allocated to Hughes Bolckow Ltd. and arrived at Blyth *16.7.1960* to be broken up.

BANFF PARK as OAKHURST   *Skyfotos*

M.36. BANFF PARK (1949 — 1950)
ON. 173264. 7133g, 4258n, 424.6 x 57.2 x 34.9 feet.
T. 3-cyl. by Dominion Engineering Works Ltd., Montreal.
9.1942: Completed by Davie Shipbuilding and Repairing Co. Ltd., Lauzon, P.Q. for Canadian Government (Park S.S. Co. Ltd managers). *8.1945:* Bareboat chartered to Ministry of War Transport (H. Hogarth and Sons managers). *4.3.1947:* Management transferred to Ohlsson S.S. Co. Ltd., Hull. *1949:* Management transferred to Joseph Constantine S.S. Line Ltd. *1950:* Sold to Rex Shipping Co. Ltd. (Hadjilias and Co. Ltd. managers), London and renamed OAKHURST. *1957:* Sold to Asturias Shipping Co. S.A., Liberia and renamed CATALUNIA. *1959:* Sold to Grenehurst Shipping Co. Ltd. (Hadjilias and Co. Ltd. managers), London. *1961:* Sold to Valia Compania Naviera S.A., Greece and renamed XENOPHON. *26.10.1962:* Grounded near Les Pierres Noires, Ushant whilst on a voyage from Cardiff to Venice with a cargo of coal and abandoned as a total loss.

INDEX